B

Today the battle has debilitating to the Church than any time since the Church was first established in the book of Acts. Believers have been fed and swallowed the lie that they are to be accepting and non-offensive to the world. This is a lie from the very pit of Hell. In fact, many believers are being persuaded they are in the faith battle alone and many even struggle with the notion as to whether faith is real or worth fighting for.

The Lord Jesus, Commander of the Heavenly Hosts, the Lion of Judah and He who comes waging war riding on a white horse out of the very throne room of heaven, has commissioned and given orders to engage the enemy through the power of the cross. Believers are not to be sitting silent, on our laurels or back peddling, allowing the enemy to take ground and, in the process, leading many souls to hell (II Tim. 2:4). Faith is the element that saves, fortifies and empowers us to engage the enemy without reserve, intimidation or fear.

BattleStrong is how we are to stand; not in our own might but in the power of the shed blood of Christ and the power of our risen Savior. Being prepared for battle and willing to wage a spiritual war is not an option for the Christ-follower, but a directive from our Lord. It is time for the Church of Christ and all individual believers to put a halt to the complacency, apathy and conformity to this world and instead to take up the armor of Christ and charge the enemy on the battlefield of this world. Too many casualties are being reported; too many warriors of the cross are falling on the mines of wickedness; and too many souls are taken prisoner while the Church of Christ takes its leisure (Eph. 6:13).

A soldier does not sit down or sit back while the enemy advances; the soldier, the infantry and the armed forces strategize, engage and conquer the enemy. I pray BattleStrong will once again remind us of our faith and the calling Christ has placed upon us as His followers. It is crucial that believers realize that our strength is only found in our faith in Christ and are willing to do whatever is necessary to fight for the preservation of such faith. Jesus said, *"Invest this for Me while I'm gone."* - Luke 19:13. War is never easy but it's time we remember that we are in an onslaught and begin fighting as if our lives and souls depend upon it - because they do and so do all of those around us.

Fight strong and in the power of Christ until He returns!

"So you, too, must keep watch! For you don't know what day your Lord is coming." - Matthew 24:42

#BattleStrong

Table of Contents

Week 1	Mustard Seeds	*Page 13*
Week 2	Unleash The Power	*Page 19*
Week 3	Faith Fight	*Page 25*
Week 4	Fleecing God	*Page 31*
Week 5	Dust To Diamonds	*Page 37*
Week 6	Divine Protection	*Page 43*
Week 7	Amazing Grace; Endless Love	*Page 49*
Week 8	Crucified With Christ	*Page 55*
Week 9	Sunbathing	*Page 63*
Week 10	Body Of Work	*Page 69*
Week 11	I Didn't Think You'd Be Here	*Page 77*
Week 12	Infiltrated By The Enemy	*Page 83*
Week 13	Get Out Of The Boat	*Page 89*
Week 14	It's Time The Church Got Angry	*Page 95*
Week 15	Give Us Our Daily Bread	*Page 103*
Week 16	It'll Only Hurt For A Few Minutes	*Page 109*
Week 17	18 Inches Of Separation	*Page 115*
Week 18	Ambassadors Of The King	*Page 121*
Week 19	Straddling The Fence	*Page 127*
Week 20	Progressive Christianity	*Page 133*
Week 21	The Man In The Mirror	*Page 141*
Week 22	Prayer Closet Conditioning	*Page 147*
Week 23	Identity Loss	*Page 153*

Week 24 A Thousand Hills Worth Of Cattle   *Page 159*

Week 25 Refined Through The Fire   *Page 167*

Week 26 The Trumpet's Blast   *Page 173*

Week 27 Waiting For The Cavalry To Arrive   *Page 181*

Week 28 Get Off God's Throne   *Page 187*

Week 29 It Only Takes A Few   *Page 193*

Week 30 The Master's Return   *Page 199*

Week 31 The Truth Whisperer   *Page 205*

Week 32 True Love Wins   *Page 211*

Week 33 Do What Matters   *Page 217*

Week 34 Then They Came For Me   *Page 223*

Week 35 Pesky Peas   *Page 231*

Week 36 Stones Of Remembrance   *Page 237*

Week 37 Praising God In The Pit   *Page 243*

Week 38 Sincere Faith   *Page 249*

Week 39 Chain Breaker   *Page 255*

Week 40 Cornerstone   *Page 261*

Week 41 Except I See   *Page 267*

Week 42 IRS (Innate Reprehensible Sin)   *Page 273*

Week 43 No Rear View Vision   *Page 281*

Week 44 300   *Page 287*

Week 45 Two Headed Piranha   *Page 295*

Week 46 Priceless   *Page 303*

Week 47 Why Me?   *Page 309*

Week 48 When The Past Comes Calling   *Page 315*

Week 49   Unanswered Prayers   *Page 321*

Week 50   Turning Lions Into Kittens   *Page 327*

Week 51   Rags To Riches   *Page 333*

Week 52   Bats In The Attic   *Page 339*

BattleStrong Testimonials

"Over the years I have been privileged to get to know Dave. He is a family man who loves God with his whole heart and wants to see his boys grow up to be men who truly chase after God's heart. Dave does not fall into the watered down manhood of America and nor does he accept it from his boys. BattleStrong will help you grow into the young adult that God wants you to be. If you believe you are where God wants you to be in your relationship with Him, then spend your time on something else; but if you are ready to be the believer God wants you to be, start reading BattleStrong today."

\- Mike Aldridge, Student Ministry Outreach Pastor

"BattleStrong has inspired my heart. In it, Dave tends to write and inform in a style that speaks to me because it takes our common problems and activities of real life and applies Scriptural advice and knowledge to them. Simply put...BattleStrong exposes the fact that we are in a battle which should not be taken lightly. One look at Dave's personal page and life and you can see that he believes that we as Christians should be "NOT just talking...but walking testimonies!" BattleStrong speaks to the fact that we CAN and DO possess the power to be strong in battle for our faith walk on this earth. I believe you will be, as I am, excited to read more BattleStrong messages."

\- Lisa Murdock Padula, Teacher/Speaker/Author/Radio Host

"*BattleStrong offers continual reminders of God's desire to get our minds off ourselves and on His faithfulness, rather than trying to live the Christian life on our own failed pursuits. BattleStrong will continually inspire you to "look to Jesus" for a fresh perspective of God's will in real life situations. You will be challenged by heroes of the faith, past and present, who overcame difficulties, failure, grief, etc. You will read of those who redirected their energies and faith to trust in God's sovereignty rather than living with their own hopelessness. This Devotional will challenge anyone seeking to more effectively live the Christian life that pleases God.*"

- Earl Thompson, Pastor

"*I have known Dave for several years now, and during that time, I have learned two things about him. First, he is a devoted husband to his wife and a loving father to his children. Second, he is devout in his faith. I believe that he is a man who loves the Lord with all of his heart, soul, and mind and loves his fellow man as our Lord has commanded. This is not only evident in his relationships with others, but also through his writings. The Lord has gifted him in that he is able to transmit deep spiritual and life-changing truths through the means of the proverbial pen. His writings have proven to be a source of blessing to me, and I believe that they will be to you as well, as we both seek daily to stay BattleStrong!*"

- H. Dwayne Spearman, Ph.D.
www.dwaynespearman.org
Founder and President, Directional Ministries

Foreword

"More than refreshing, rather more like a renewal – that is the sense I get each time I read BattleStrong! There are times that the scriptures and anecdotes paired together by author, Dave Frett, are like a tall cool drink on a hot summer day. He often brings the power of God's word to you framed by manifestation known to be of God – too deep and wide to measure. I encourage you to keep this book nearby. Allow your heart and your mind to be challenged anew, and reminded of our Heavenly Father's proximity. Get ready to be encouraged, not for encouragement's sake, rather to spur others on in their life journey. This book will serve you well as food and drink, as well as ammunition and weaponry against the attacks of Satan to discourage you. Defeat will be staved off when you are BATTLESTRONG!"

- Don Meckley, Pastor

✝

Week 1
MUSTARD
SEEDS

The apostles said to the Lord, "Show us how to increase our faith." The Lord answered, "If you had faith even as small as a mustard seed, you could say to this mulberry tree, 'May you be uprooted and be planted in the sea,' and it would obey you!
- Luke 17:5-6

For 10 years missionaries Robert and Mary Moffat labored faithfully in Bechuanaland (now called Botswana) without one ounce of encouragement to lighten their load. They were not able to report a single convert in all that time. Finally the directors of their mission board began to question the wisdom of continuing the work. The thought of leaving this land, however, brought great despair and agony to the souls of this dedicated couple, for they felt sure that God was in their labors and that they would soon see people turn to Christ. They remained steadfast and secure in this foreign land; and for a year or two longer, darkness prevailed. Then one day a friend in England sent a message to the Moffats. She wanted to mail them a gift and asked what they would like. Trusting that in time the Lord would reward their efforts, Mrs. Moffat replied, *"Send us a communion set; I am sure it will soon be needed."* God honored that believing woman's faith. The Holy Spirit soon moved upon the hearts of the community and soon a little group of six converts formed the first Christian church in that country. The communion set from England had been held up in the mail but on the very day before the first memorial service of the Lord's super in Bechuanaland, the set arrived.

Faith is a mighty weapon; it will change one's life and it will alter the direction of a people.

Faith is a mighty weapon; it will change one's life and it will alter the direction of a people. On multiple occasions Jesus reminded the disciples if they had but the faith of a mustard seed nothing was beyond their grasp. Jesus was attempting to teach the disciples that He did not expect them to have astounding levels of faith but that, just as a mustard seed was the smallest of all seeds in that region of the world, with minimal faith in Him, the world was their oyster. Whether Jesus was telling the disciples that mountains or rooted trees would actually get up and move at their command is beyond our knowing; but what we do know about His teaching is that if they but believed in and trusted Him, that there was no stopping the mighty acts they could perform in His name. In Hebrews 11:1 faith has been described for us as, *"the reality of what we hope for; it is the evidence of things we cannot see."* Think about it from this perspective for a moment – when one sits down in a chair, do they first lift it up, inspecting the sturdiness or the strength of the legs, or do they just sit down, presuming it will hold their body? Faith is demonstrating trust in someone or something that you cannot prove. A central difference between science and faith is that faith says, *"God said it, I believe it"* whereas science attempts to prove why or why not a particular thought or concept should be believed. Hence, the essence of faith is found in child-like acceptance.

Children have no adversity to believing what they are taught. If a parent says, *"Jump. I'll catch you"*, the child does not begin to think *"Let me determine the height I'm at, the speed I'll come crashing down, the injuries I may incur or doubt the ability of my parent to catch me"*. They simply jump and enjoy the ride. In fact, the story is told how one night a house caught fire and a young boy was forced to flee to the roof. The father stood on the ground below with outstretched arms, calling to his son, *"Jump! I'll catch you."* He knew the boy had to jump to save his life. All the boy could see, however, was flame, smoke and blackness. As can be imagined, he was afraid to leave the roof. His father kept yelling: *"Jump! I will catch you."* But the boy protested, *"Daddy, I can't see you."* The father replied, *"But I can see you and that's all that matters."* This my friends is a perfect illustration of the faith we must have in our God; though we cannot see Him, He can see us and that's all that matters!

In John 20 we read the story of Jesus' appearing to the disciples after His resurrection and, specifically to Thomas. Though this was not the first appearing of Jesus to the disciples since His resurrection, it was the first time Thomas was present. It is no secret that Thomas had before exclaimed that, *"I won't believe it unless I see the nail wounds in his hands, put my fingers into them, and place my hand into the wound in his side."* – John 20:25. It is evident that Thomas was lacking in the faith department but who could blame him? He had witnessed Jesus' death and burial, and even though he knew Jesus' words that He would rise the third day, it was still a bit to swallow. However, Jesus in His love and compassion, and His desire to see Thomas believe and be restored, graciously responded, *"Put your finger here, and look at my hands. Put your hand into the wound in my side. Don't be faithless any longer. Believe!"* – John 20:27.

The question this leads all of us to ask ourselves today is, what kind of faith do I have? Do I have a lack of faith as did Thomas or do I have the faith of a mustard seed which Jesus described as making all things possible. Let us claim the promise and blessing as Jesus declared to Thomas when He said, *"You believe because you have seen me. Blessed are those who believe without seeing me."* – John 20:29. Begin today growing your mustard seed.

Food for Thought

In which areas of my life do I need to have more faith?
I.e. Family, finances, health, etc.

_____

_____

_____

_____

_____

If I truly believed God would answer my prayers, what would
I want ask of Him?

_____

_____

_____

_____

Is my faith growing daily? Why or why not?

_____

_____

_____

_____

_____

How can I 'grow' my faith from a mustard seed to a mountain daily?

_____

_____

_____

_____

_____

Faith is an offensive weapon not a defensive strategy. How can I put faith to work in my life today to give me greater victory?

_____

_____

_____

_____

_____

✝

Week 2
UNLEASH THE POWER

Do not quench the Spirit.
- I Thessalonians 5:19

What would be your response if I showed up with a brand new 2016 Ferrari California, fully gassed, engine purring and handed you the title? Would this magnificent beast, listed at $202,000, stocked with 553-hp allowing you to go from 0-62 in 3.6 seconds with a top speed of 196mph become your most prized possession? Or would you simply take it home and store it in the garage afraid to scratch it, crash it or run out of gas? Would you attempt to sell it before you put any mileage on it, thereby driving down its value? Or would you find the first straight open highway and test out the full potential of this magnificent beast? This my friends is often the way that we respond to the indwelling of the Holy Ghost. For whatever reason we are afraid or unwilling to let the Spirit loose. Instead we hamper, squelch and even extinguish the power in our hands; the power that affords us the ability to race through life, crossing the finish line, only to see the victory flags being waved in our rear view mirrors.

The Spirit may become squelched in the believer's life through many different avenues – from allowing the hardening of our hearts where we are no longer tender to the still, soft words of God; to disobeying the instructions of God given in His Word; to forgetting the sin we have been saved from, causing our hearts and lives to be puffed up in arrogance and pride. In fact, C. T. Studd, the famous missionary to China in the late 1800's-early 1900's, has expressed it as, *"How little chance the Holy Spirit has nowadays. The churches and missionary societies have so bound Him in red tape that they practically ask Him to sit in a corner while they do the work themselves."* Do we really believe we can do the work of God apart from God?

As believers we possess a power so strong that if fully unleashed would change this world forever; but before changing the world, it would change our lives!

In Ephesians 4:30, Paul gives a stern admonition about quenching the Spirit when he says, *"And do not bring sorrow to God's Holy Spirit by the way you live. Remember, he has identified you as his own, guaranteeing that you will be saved on the day of redemption."* Thinking back to the free Ferrari that was hypothetically delivered to you earlier, would it be possible to test the limits of its power if you were afraid to place your foot on the gas pedal? With regard to handling turns and slippery roads, how would one perform if he did not practice? And on that rare occasion, if something went wrong, how would you know it if you'd never opened the instruction manual? Our lives, riding in the Ferrari, will never reach the greatest potential and end result if we don't punch the gas and let the Holy Spirit power us.

As believers we possess a power so strong that if fully unleashed would change this world forever; but before changing the world, it would change our lives! D. L. Moody once noted, *"The world has yet to see what God can do with a man fully consecrated to him. By God's help, I aim to be that man."* Moody understood that in order to be that man he would need to unleash the power of God, but in order for the power of God to be unleashed in his life he would first need to get out of God's way and just let Him work.

From a practical perspective, I'm sure many have used a fire before - either camping or to heat one's house. In both ways, when one is attempting to get the embers bright and hot, he does not throw water on it. Quite honestly, a lot of 'pampering' goes into the start of a fire; ensuring the twigs are of good burning consistency, using lighter fluid to help ignite the flames and then making sure the wind does not snuff out the young flames - to knowing exactly the right time to add the logs for the long burn. The Christian life is much the same way. When we first get saved we're excited, we're amped; but then we allow the winds of this world to blow out the initial spark. Instead of adding more kindling to the fire, we allow the rain to fall and smolder our once vibrant flame. Even worse, sometimes the strong winds and drowning rainfall come from fellow believers; those who have allowed the once hot and ferocious flames of their lives to become but a flicker and now refuse to accept the enthusiasm in another.

In the early years after Christ's death, burial, resurrection and ascension the world was turned upside down by twelve men; not the most educated, not the most polished, not the most eloquent of speakers - simply twelve men that had a fire burning deep and strong within their souls. Men that had experienced the power of God's Spirit and were now willing to make a difference, an indelible mark on this world that would stand the test of time.

Today's world is cold and calloused and in need of the fire from Heaven. We that claim the name of Jesus Christ possess that fire deep in our souls; the question is whether we're going to let it burn bright or cover it until it burns out?

Christians, stop keeping your Ferrari in the garage! It's time to take it out for a run. The Holy Spirit is just waiting to be unleashed so that He can work in you and through you.

Food for Thought

Does the Holy Ghost power my faith or is my faith run on self-propulsion? If self, how can I strengthen my faith and unleash the Spirit's power in my life?

_____

_____

_____

_____

_____

How am I stifling the Holy Ghost in my life? I.e. Doubt? Walking in the flesh? Lack of time in the word and prayer? Filling my mind/eyes/ears with corrupt things?

_____

_____

_____

_____

_____

How can I live out my faith and give God unlimited control of my life?

_____

_____

_____

_____

_____

How can I improve my 'spiritual muscle' so as to be the high performance 'Christian' God wants me to be?

_____

_____

_____

_____

_____

Oftentimes we complain that it appears God isn't working in our lives. On the other hand, God has expectations of a believer's life in order to be usable. If I was to honesty look at my life from God's perspective, would I use myself? If so, what am I doing right? If not, why?

_____

_____

_____

_____

_____

✝

Week 3
FAITH FIGHT

Fight the good fight for the true faith. Hold tightly to the eternal life to which God has called you, which you have declared so well before many witnesses.
- I Timothy 6:12

The story is told how the famous first American Heavy Weight Champion boxer, John L. Sullivan, was asked why he had never taken to giving boxing lessons.

Sullivan responded, *"Well, son, I tried it once"*. He further went on to say, *"A husky young man took one lesson from me and went home a little the worse for wear. When he came around for his second lesson he said: 'Mr. Sullivan, it was my idea to learn enough about boxing from you to be able to lick a certain young gentleman that I've got it in for. But I've changed my mind'. 'If it's all the same to you, Mr. Sullivan, I'll send this young gentleman down here to take the rest of my lessons for me.'"*

How often do we feel like this? We want God to teach us

how to fight in order to be prepared for the enemy. But we're afraid to learn the lessons or to take the licks it requires to become a champ. In fact, our whole disposition changes; we allow ourselves to steep into a feeling that God is just looking for a reason to deny our requests or to put us through the ringer. However, we forget that in order to be prepared for the twelve round bout we must first put in the work. A poem that was once written called, *Everything I Needed*, describes the fight preparation as,

> *I asked for strength and*
> *God gave me difficulties to make me strong.*
>
> *I asked for wisdom and*
> *God gave me problems to solve.*
>
> *I asked for prosperity and*
> *God gave me brawn and brains to work.*
>
> *I asked for courage and*
> *God gave me dangers to overcome.*
>
> *I asked for patience and*
> *God placed me in situations where I was forced to wait.*
>
> *I asked for love and*
> *God gave me troubled people to help.*
>
> *I asked for favors and*
> *God gave me opportunities.*

I received nothing I wanted
I received everything I needed.

My prayers have all been answered.

If we desire to be champions; if we desire to not be sifted; and if we desire to stand strong against the attacks of the enemy, then it's probably time we stop taking the fight so lightly and realize it's not a game. The enemy is well aware of the gravity of the situation. It's a fight and he's not holding anything back; he's coming at us with everything he's got and its time we stop just blocking his punches and started throwing some of our own.

Recently the world lost a boxing icon in Muhammad Ali. Regardless of his political or religious beliefs, from a purely athletic and competitive standpoint, he was a giant. The reason for this was: he trained hard, was willing to learn from every punch taken and believed in his ability. As believers in the hardest and toughest fight of our lives, the faith fight, we need to believe in the One that strengthens us, prepares us, and teaches us – our Trainer, Jesus Christ. The Christian life is not for the weak of mind, body or soul.

Being a huge fan of the Rocky movie series, I am inspired particularly from the scene in Rocky IV where Sylvester Stallone's character, Rocky Balboa, goes to Siberia to prepare for his fight against the physically freakish Russian, Ivan Drago. He does not train in the usual gym through the usual means; the fight is with an unusual opponent which requires abnormal training. The training requires isolation from the public and news media; the training requires amassing a level of strength never before gained; and the training requires new and strategic tactics. The reason for all of this – his very life hangs in the balance.

As believers, our lives hang in the balance of the faith fight we are battling. This is not a publicity fight as between Rocky and Thunderlips (Hulk Hogan) in Rocky III. In fact, the fight could end up with same end result as the fight in Rocky V between Drago and Apollo Creed. Apollo lost his life because he was overmatched and unprepared. Apollo did not take seriously the threat of Drago as so many Christians fail to take serious the threat of Satan. Instead of training for the fight, Apollo treated it like a circus, as entertainment and mocked the intensity of his opponent.

Today believers dance around the issues, fail to throw any intentional, and productive shots at the enemy and take it across the chin regularly. The faith fight has merely become a publicity stunt designed to prove to the world we are not serious and that the fight is purely for entertainment purposes. However, the fight is real; the devil's goal is to not only knock us out, but to annihilate us. The twelfth round is upon us; the Church is against the ropes; and the enemy is looking for the final punch. What will we do to prevent being knocked down and out? What are we willing to do to battle back and rip the potential victory from the enemy's grasp? As was written in Jude 1:3, we ought to *urge you to defend the faith that God has entrusted once for all time to his holy people.*

The fight's not over. There's still time to mount a comeback; but it will require a change of mentality, a change of will and a change of spirit. Fight on friend! The bell hasn't sounded.

Food for Thought

Am I actively engaged in the faith fight? Am I daily standing strong or have I been facing defeats? Where? Why?

_____

_____

_____

_____

Am I learning the lessons in each 'round' that will strengthen my faith and allow me to finish strong and win? What faith lessons have I recently learned?

_____

_____

_____

_____

_____

_____

How am I demonstrating I understand the severity of the faith fight I'm in? How can I better train to be prepared for what lies ahead?

_____

_____

_____

_____

_____

List my 'training regimen' and ask God to show me where and how I can improve.

_____

_____

_____

_____

_____

Am I fighting the battle alone or am I flanked by fellow 'warriors'? Accountability is key for success. Who is in my accountability circle? Does it need to change?

_____

_____

_____

_____

_____

Week 4
FLEECING GOD

Gideon replied, "If you are truly going to help me, show me a sign to prove that it is really the Lord speaking to me."
- Judges 6:17

It is noted that Hudson Taylor was so weak in the final months of his life that he mentioned to a dear friend, *"I'm so weak that I can't work or read my Bible and I can hardly pray. I can only lie still in God's arms like a little child and trust."* Have you ever felt this way? Has this been an experienced emotion when God has called you to a specific mission? Have you ever felt so weak, discouraged, unprepared or insignificant that you doubted God's ability to use YOU? Fear not friend, many a child of God has found himself in the same or similar situations. God has over and over again shown why He called them and why He has called you.

In the book of Judges, we read a story about a common man named Gideon. Even while Gideon could not possibly understand why God had commissioned him and/or how God would use him to bring deliverance to His people, God had everything in hand. In fact, Gideon was so suspicious that he was actually hearing from God Himself, that he felt compelled to test God – not just once mind you, but twice.

Quite possibly one reason why Gideon failed to take God at His word was not because he doubted that God could fulfill His end of the bargain. But because Gideon had no belief in himself; to say he lacked confidence would be an understatement. Gideon was not a bad guy, in fact, he was a lot like many of us – insecure, indecisive and reluctant. What if he failed? What if this was not really God's plan? What if he was attempting this act in his own strength or to embolden his own reputation? The entire nation of Israel rested upon his shoulders and the success of this endeavor. No pressure.

As the story continues, we see that Gideon would put God to the test. Gideon desired to know that beyond a shadow of a doubt, God was working and God would bring about the victory. He realized he was an inferior and broken vessel, and was completely incapable of such a great task apart from God. So one night before bed, Gideon put his rug out on the front steps. His goal – to have God wet the rug with dew while ensuring everything else remained dry. Low and behold, the following morning when Gideon awoke, and he went to check on the rug, everything was as he had requested of God. The rug was not just a little wet – it was soaking wet. In fact, Gideon was able to wring it out to which it filled a bowl. *"Amazing! God has answered just as I asked"*, he must have thought. While this was a terrific assurance to Gideon, it just wasn't quite enough ...not yet.

So once again the following night Gideon sought God to show him a sign that this project he had called him to was really ordained by Him. This time Gideon would once again place his rug out on the front steps, but this time instead of asking God to wet the rug while all the ground remained dry, Gideon requested that God would keep the rug dry while wetting everything else.

As the sun began to rise, Gideon leaped from his bed and ran to the front door. As he swung it open and peered down at the rug he had put out that night, he discovered it was as dry as a cactus in the middle of the desert. Not only was the rug barren dry, but the ground was wet everywhere he looked. God had once again answered his prayer just as he had asked. It was now that Gideon knew His God, the only true God, the God of Israel had truly called him to make a difference in the lives of His people. The time for testing and the time for doubting needed to cease. Now was the time to believe and take God at His word.

Today the concept of fleecing has taken on a very negative connotation. In fact, today the dictionary defines fleecing as, 'to gain a great deal of money from someone, usually by overcharging or cheating them'. However, in Gideon's day, the act of 'fleecing' was a demonstration of God's commitment to empower His man to fulfill His work.

How many times in our own lives do we test God? Sometimes we may not even conscientiously be aware of the test while at other times it is completely intentional. So what does God's word say about putting God to the test? Well I Peter 5:7, tells us to, *"Give all your worries and cares to God, for he cares about you."* How much anxiety must Gideon have been experiencing? A common man, threshing wheat at the bottom of a winepress while attempting to hide from his enemies, was now being called by God to lead His nation in a military campaign to bring relief and freedom from barbaric oppression. God completely understood and not only was He not angry or annoyed but He answered just as asked. So as to build this man and help him to understand he would not be alone but that God would be the One to bring the victory.

Many Christians wonder why God is able to use one person but not another. Well A. W. Tozer once wrote, *"Why do some persons 'find' God in a way others do not? Why does God manifest His Presence to some and let multitudes of others struggle along in the half-light of imperfect Christian experience? Of course the will of God is the same for all. He has no favorites within His household. All He has ever done for any of His children, He will do for all of His children. The difference lies not with God but with us."*

In the end, for Gideon, for Thomas, and for us, God desires we not be faithless and doubting but that we be sure and secure of His working in our life. If we need to beseech Him to prove to us that He has called us to a great work, He says, *"Come"*. God taught Gideon to trust Him but He also taught Gideon it was acceptable to confirm what he thought to be the case.

Today if you feel God is calling you to a particular work but you're not sure, put the fleece out and watch how He answers your petition.

Food for Thought

Have I ever felt God was leading in a particular area but I was unsure how to confirm it? Have I felt like I would be wrong to question God? How have I brought closure or certainty to such situations?

_____

_____

_____

_____

_____

Am I allowing the 'enemy' to cause me doubt and discouragement in questioning whether God can use me? Based upon scripture, what verses confirm that God CAN and WANTS to use me?

_____

_____

_____

_____

_____

List three prayers that God has recently answered. If God has answered these requests, why am I still doubting God will answer my other requests?

_____

_____

_____

_____

Name a current 'fleece' in my own life that I am desiring God to answer. Is my faith strong enough to believe God will answer and then step out in faith? Explain.

_____

_____

_____

_____

How can my faith life be that of the Gideon who led 300 men and defeated an entire nation rather than the Gideon who found himself hiding in a winepress for fear of the enemy?

_____

_____

_____

_____

✝

Week 5
DUST TO DIAMONDS

*Dear brothers and sisters, when troubles of any kind
come your way, consider it an opportunity for great
joy. For you know that when your faith is tested,
your endurance has a chance to grow. So let it grow,
for when your endurance is fully developed, you
will be perfect and complete, needing nothing.*
- James 1:2-4

Recently I heard a joke that paints a clear picture of how life
can change on a dime. After some nagging discomfort a man
finally decided to see his doctor. After a lengthy check-up,
inclusive of a panel of tests, the doctor returned to give the
man his diagnosis. As the doctor entered the room he said
to the man, *"I have bad news and I have worse news. Which
would you like first?"* As the color quickly faded from the man's
face, he responded, *"Let's have the bad news first."* Softly and
compassionately the doctor explained, *"The bad news is you only
have 24 hours to live."* Completely at a loss for words the man
responded, *"I can't imagine what would be worse than that."* After

a minute or so the doctor replied, *"I forgot to tell you yesterday."*

How often are we seemingly besieged by unexpected vats of bad news? Possibly after balancing the check book and having to rob Peter to pay Paul, we find out that the car needs a new set of tires; maybe the kids need new shoes because the family pet decided to play catch with them; or possibly the fridge decides to go on the fritz. Maybe the level of news is even more extreme. It could be you find out your company is downsizing and you will be one of the casualties or, like the man in the illustration, a serious health concern is unexpectedly discovered. Whatever the trial, the fear and anxiety produced is real. However, as believers there is often more to learn than what appears on the surface.

The faith of a believer is designed to strengthen under pressure. Much like a lump of coal is transformed into a priceless diamond under extreme heat and pressure, so does the faith of a believer in the midst of trials. C.S. Lewis once commented, *"Hardships often prepare ordinary people for an extraordinary destiny."*

Diamonds have become one of the most valued gifts in the world. A diamond can range in price from a few hundred dollars to millions. The most expensive diamond on record that can be valued is a Cullinan Diamond reportedly estimated to cost $400 million, while the top two diamonds are literally priceless. Diamonds signify the love between two people and diamonds signify a top tier achiever – in business, in marriage and in life. Many women long to have diamond rings, necklaces and ear rings – and the bigger the better. But what is often neglected and forgotten is that the more stupendous the diamond, the more extensive the ordeal to produce it; the hotter the heat it endured; and the greater the intensity to produce the pressure.

A believer's life is like that of a diamond. Before Christ takes over, his life is like a lump of coal – dirty, dark and worthless; but once Christ enters and the trials come, He uses the pressure to conform one to His image. Many a Christian desires his life to be the biggest and most brilliant of diamonds, but he will also be the first to complain when the trials come that create the pressure that generates the exquisite beauty yet to be revealed.

In the believer's life, there is no 'maybe' and/or 'what if' struggles will come – it is an absolute in this life we live. However, in today's passage we read about the attitude we should possess as we embrace the difficulties. In fact, James says we should have *"great joy"* in the storms of life. Great joy? How could anyone possibly enjoy or relish tumultuous events of life? You mean I should be happy when sickness attacks my family? I should praise God when financial hardships come my way? And I should be excited to entertain such drowning dilemmas? How is this possible?

The process will never be easy but the end result will always be worth the pain. In I Peter 4:12-13 we read, *"Dear friends, don't be surprised at the fiery trials you are going through, as if something strange were happening to you. Instead, be very glad—for these trials make you partners with Christ in his suffering, so that you will have the wonderful joy of seeing his glory when it is revealed to all the world."* Additionally, Paul encouraged us in Romans 5:3, when he wrote, *"We can rejoice, too, when we run into problems and trials, for we know that they help us develop endurance."* The process of diamond crafting is not a quick process – it requires time, effort and hard work, but so does our Christian walk. To behold such an elegant and refined jewel requires breaking, forming, shaping and polishing; whether a diamond or the believer's life. Charles Spurgeon once described it as, *"Whenever God means to make a man great, He always breaks him into pieces first".*

The difference between coal and diamonds is the purity of the element. Diamonds are pure, while coal possesses impurities; such can be the correlation between the world and God's children. Those who know not Christ are impure, filled with all kinds of pollutants – while the believer is pure because of his Spirit filled existence. Therefore, once we accept Christ as Savior we are immediately transformed from coal to diamonds. It is then that the diamond cutting begins taking place.

Be encouraged Saint! As A.W. Tozer once noted, *"God never uses anyone greatly until He tests them deeply."* If you are being tested today then you are being refined for His service. Christ is preparing you for great things – the greatest of which is being conformed to His image. Remember, as Darlene Sala once remarked, *"God has formed many diamonds but He made only one you. You are unique."* You are loved. You are a diamond.

Food for Thought

Does my faith life reflect a brilliant diamond or a mere piece of coal? How can my faith life become the diamond it's meant to be?

_____

_____

_____

_____

_____

When fear knocks at life's door, does faith answer? Why or why not?

_____

_____

_____

_____

Just as pressure is used to form a diamond, what specific 'pressure' is occurring in my life? Am I thankful for it or do I simply complain?

_____

_____

_____

_____

Many believers desire God to use them but are unwilling to endure the preparation. Do I ask God to 'prepare' me or and I content to remain 'on the sideline?' Explain.

_____

_____

_____

_____

_____

What pollutants are presently in my faith life? Am I interested in having my faith life 'cleaned up'? How am I asking the Great Physician to heal me?

_____

_____

_____

_____

_____

_____

_____

_____

DIVINE PROTECTION

*What shall we say about such wonderful things as
these? If God is for us, who can ever be against us?*
- Romans 8:31

Has it ever occurred to you how many times you have been
spared harm or possible death on a daily basis? Maybe it was
being delayed five minutes that prevented you from being in
a deadly car accident. Maybe it was slipping on an ice patch
to only fall and smack your rear end instead of your head.
Maybe it was accidentally ingesting the wrong medicine that
could have caused a life ending allergic reaction. Maybe it was
in your younger years of horseplay and antics. Regardless the
circumstances, God daily provides His protection in and over
our lives to protect us from life and ourselves.

I once heard a story about God's divine protection for a
missionary family in South Africa. The story is told from the
wife's perspective as she describes how in the early days of her
husband's service, he surrendered to go to the mission field. She

went on to say, how after he had finished raising his support, they were soon packed and flying across the ocean to the shores of Africa. As they landed in a large city on the banks of the Congo River, they flew over the jungles and African bush, and the muddy rivers on their way to the mission point out in the African bush.

As fate would have it, one day their little son and his friends were out scouring for meat. They spotted some birds in a tree off to the side of the trail. As they were slowly creeping along this little, narrow footpath, quietly trying to get closer to the birds, all the time continuing to watch the birds in the tree instead of watching the pathway they were sneaking up on, the boy stepped right on a deadly Black Mamba snake, one of the most deadly snakes in the Bush.

However, just before the boy stepped on the snake, the Lord had sent a protective device - a bush rat. Additionally, God had aroused the snake's appetite, as the snake had just caught the rat and was slowly swallowing it as the boy stepped directly on it.

The rat was about half way down the snake's throat while half of the rat was still hanging out of the snake's mouth. Fortunately, when the snake reared up and struck him on the knee, the snake's fangs could not pierce the boy's skin. The boy and his little African friends quickly killed the snake and everyone was left unharmed. A comment that exemplifies this story was spoken by Warren Wiersbe when he said, *"The safest place in all the world is in the will of God, and the safest protection in all the world is the name of God."*

Just as this little boy and his family were protected from seemingly a painful and rather quick death, God has demonstrated and promised His protection to all of His children. In Acts 12:6-17, we read of how Peter was rescued from prison and imminent death at the hands of a cruel and ruthless Herod by the angel of the Lord. The Bible tells us how the Church had been praying for him and how God had sent His very own angel to protect and release him from the dark and dingy prison cell. This divine protection was so miraculous that, even though the Church had been praying for his release, when Peter showed up at the house of a fellow Saint, there was great surprise and disbelief. This is an example by which Billy Graham spoke when he said, *"God's angels often protect his servants from potential enemies."*

If it were made known to us how frequently we are surrounded and kept safe through the divine protection of our God, it would leave us dumbfounded and in awe. Picture a person with jaw dropping effects and that is how we would appear with such knowledge.

As we walk through life let us not be careless but let us also not walk in fear. While we do not know what lies around the next bend, we do know that we walk not alone. God is there before us, He is with us each step of the way, and He has brought us through each previous step of life. What reason do we have to not believe He will carry and protect us today? As John Newton was once quoted, *"Through many dangers, toils and* snares, I have already come; 'Tis grace has brought me safe thus far and grace will lead me home."

Let us thank God today for His divine protection over our lives!

Food for Thought

Describe a time where if not for Divine intervention, life's circumstances may have proved deadly for me.

_____

_____

_____

_____

_____

Take a moment and think about the spiritual realm which we cannot see. The Bible describes it as _"spiritual forces of evil in the heavenly places"_ - Ephesians 6:12. Imagine and note what I believe I'd see if for a moment God allowed me to see into that realm. NOTE: The reason this is important is that everything we see is dictated by what we can't see.

_____

_____

_____

_____

_____

How can I keep my eyes on the eternal rather than the temporal thereby strengthening my faith? (Matt. 6:19-21).

_____

_____

_____

_____

_____

Am I by faith following God's will or am I trying to float outside of it? If so, what do I need to do in order to be safely in His will?

_____

_____

_____

_____

_____

_____

_____

_____

_____

Week 7
AMAZING GRACE; ENDLESS LOVE

We love each other because he loved us first.
- I John 4:19

Once in church, I heard a story about the rivalry between the 19th century preachers, Charles Spurgeon and Joseph Parker. One particular story described how Parker spoke about the poor condition of children living in Spurgeon's orphanage. One day it was shared with Spurgeon how Parker had ridiculed the condition of the orphanage. This action agitated Spurgeon so he thundered back at Parker the very next week from his pulpit. The entire message and response to Parker was printed in the papers and quickly became the talk of the town. People came from near and far by the masses to Parker's church, the very next Sunday, to hear how he would respond. Parker would proceed to say, *"I understand Dr. Spurgeon is not in his pulpit today, and this is the Sunday they use to take an offering for the orphanage. I suggest we take a love offering here instead."* The crowd was astonished but delighted. Immediately at the end of the service a collection was taken up and the ushers actually had to empty the plates on 3 separate occasions. During the week Spurgeon felt the need to clear the air with Parker. As he showed up and knocked on the door of Parker's office, Spurgeon proclaimed, *"You know Parker, you have practiced grace on me. You have given me not what I deserved, you have given me what I needed."*

Have we ever stopped to consider that this is an example of what God has done for us? He has withheld from us what we are deserving of and in its place has given us what we needed. Grace has often been spelled out in the acronym form as God's Riches at Christ's Expense. This is so awesomely true! Much like this illustration we were filthy beggars, not able to provide for ourselves and without a home or a future. Then Christ. In all actuality, that is all that needs to be said...then Christ. Oh, the love one must have to exhibit such grace.

The old faithful hymn, Amazing Grace, tells the story of its author John Newton. Born in London on July 24, 1725, Newton was the son of a single parent merchant ship Commander as his mother had died early in his childhood years. At the ripe young age of eleven, he went to sea with his father for a total of six trips before his father retired. With the knowledge of the seas and the seas alone, Newton took on service as part of a man-of-war. Unfortunately, the conditions did not serve him well and instead of attempting to change things or bear with them, he deserted. Once he was found and captured, he was publicly flogged and demoted from midshipman to a common seaman. At some point down the line he was transferred to a slave ship where he would reside off the coast of Sierra Leone before becoming the servant of a slave trader. While in this position he was brutally abused until at the meager age of 23, he was rescued by a friend of his father who was also a sea captain. After Newton physically and mentally healed he became a captain of his own ship which would transport slaves. One night, on a voyage home, the ship entered a horrific storm which made it near impossible to steer the ship. It was on this night he would record in his journal the following words, *"Lord, have mercy upon us"*. It was through this situation that God began to work on Newton's heart showing him firsthand what grace and love truly meant.

We are so undeserving of such love and grace but that is what makes it so special. John Newton is not an anomaly, he is a depiction of each and every one of us. In so being, amazing grace and endless love are best defined in the example of Jesus described in Romans 5:7-9, *"Now, most people would not be willing to die for an upright person, though someone might perhaps be willing to die for a person who is especially good. But God showed his great love for us by sending Christ to die for us while we were still sinners. And since we have been made right in God's sight by the blood of Christ, he will certainly save us from God's condemnation."*

While God has most certainly demonstrated grace to us, and does so continually each day, we are also not to take it for granted. We should every day give thanks and strive to become more like Christ. Grace does not give us a license to do wrong, but quite the opposite, it should compel us to allow the Holy Spirit to mold and transform us into what Christ would have us become. Grace alleviates the need for perfection but also provides the strength and determination to revolutionize our lives. No longer do we have to be beaten down, knowing and being constantly reminded that we are sinful men, but because of Christ's amazing grace and endless love we have a shining and illuminated future to not only live for Christ but to share the redemptive story of our lives with others for their good and God's glory. Just as John Newton went on to become a minister of the Word, demonstrating that because of the amazing grace shown him nothing was beyond the scope of God, so too our lives can be a clean chalkboard, waiting to have God write a new storyline that will depict His perfect will for our lives.

Food for Thought

Describe and reflect upon a time where God miraculously stretched my faith and provided a need that was beyond my control. What was significant about it? Did I give God the proper and due praise and thanksgiving for my blessing?

_____

_____

_____

_____

_____

_____

_____

God has demonstrated more mercy and grace to me than I have ever deserved. Is there someone in my life that I am withholding the same from? What do I need to do to make it right?

_____

_____

_____

_____

_____

Living under grace does not give me a license to sin. How can I ask God to help me avoid abusing grace in order to sin and instead use grace to testify of His healing power in my life?

_____

_____

_____

_____

_____

Using grace as the focal point, write a few lines that capture God's grace at work in my life.

_____

_____

_____

_____

_____

Take a few minutes to thank God for His amazing grace and never ending love. Optional: share with others.

✝

Week 8
CRUCIFIED
WITH CHRIST

My old self has been crucified with Christ. It is no longer I who live, but Christ lives in me. So I live in this earthly body by trusting in the Son of God, who loved me and gave himself for me.
- Galatians 2:20

Have you ever thought what it must have felt like to be crucified? How Christ suffered and anguished on the cross? The crucifixion was one of the most horrid forms of execution throughout history. Prior to the actual act of being nailed to the cross, the individual would face a number of pre-cross beatings. In regard to Jesus, after a mock trial in which false witnesses were called against Him, inevitably leading to the decree by Pontius Pilot to condemn Him to death, Jesus suffered immensely. The first tortuous act He would live through was a beating from a Roman soldier using a flag rum of flagellum which consisted of small pieces of bone and metal attached to a number of leather strands. The maximum number of lashes was set at 39 by Jewish law, even though the Romans had no max, because anything past 39 generally was a death warrant in itself. The actual lashing would strip the skin from the recipient's back, exposing a bloody mass of muscle and bone. Needless to say, this kind of whipping would cause an extreme loss of blood, most likely weakening the victim even to the point of unconsciousness.

After sustaining this graphic beating Jesus was then stripped down naked in public, would have a scarlet robe placed on Him and would have a crown of thorns thrust into his scalp causing blood to come streaming down His face. Unlike rose thorns that we are accustomed to here in the United States, these thorns were more than likely 1 to 2 inches long. As the soldiers then continued to beat Jesus in the head, this would cause the thorns to drive down deeper into His scalp causing severe bleeding. Additionally, these soldiers continued to mock Him, (ripping His beard from His face to the point that the Bible says He could not even be recognized as a man) spitting in His face and casting lots for His garments.

It was now time for Jesus to walk the road to Calvary.

The path He would walk was known as the Via Dolorosa or the *"way of suffering"*. This path was estimated to be 650 yards in which He was forced to carry the crossbar which weighed between 80 and 110 pounds. Imagine having to carry anything after already experiencing such a beating, let alone something that weighed so much! At some point down the path Jesus fell due to the weight of the crossbar and the complete exhaustion and pain He was feeling. During this fall it is believed that

Jesus may have suffered a contusion of the heart which could have left Him predisposed to a rupture of the heart while hanging on the cross.

The time had now come for the crucifixion itself. The process of the crucifixion was perfected by the Romans to inflict maximum and long-term pain. The site of crucifixions was outside the city limits since it was quite unsanitary as the body was often left to rot on the cross. It also was not out of the norm for the individual to be eaten alive while still on the cross by wild beasts. At the onset of the crucifixion Jesus was laid on the patibulum while 7-inch-long, 3/8 inch round nails were driven into His wrists. The nails would sever the median nerve which would cause shocks of pain to radiate throughout His arms. The patibulum was then lifted up and placed on the stipes which was approximately 7 feet high at which time the feet were nailed to the stipes. The knees were bent and placed into a very uncomfortable position making it difficult for long-term push-ups to draw breath into the body for a desired result of asphyxiation.

When one begins to understand the love that Christ demonstrated to us in order to voluntarily experience such grave torture, it should compel us to aspire toward a new, active and vibrant devotion to Him.

Ultimately, Jesus suffered from severe hypovolemia from loss of blood (dehydration) which would lead to death from lung collapse, decreased oxygen while experiencing an increase of carbon dioxide, fluids building up in the lungs to cause drowning, with the end result being heart failure due to enormous levels of stress.

When one begins to understand the love that Christ demonstrated toward us in order to voluntarily experience such grave torture, it should compel us to aspire toward a new, active and vibrant devotion to Him. In Galatians 2:20, Paul reveals to us that the least we can do is to live for the One who was willing to die for us. Such love not only demands, but should elicit, radical obedience through every outlet of our lives. When asked what radical obedience should look like from a believer, David Platt uttered, *"Radical obedience to Christ is not easy... It's not comfort, not health, not wealth and not prosperity in this world. Radical obedience to Christ risks losing all these things. But in the end, such risk finds its reward in Christ. And He is more than enough for us."*

Years after Jesus' death, burial, resurrection and ascension to Heaven, as Peter was being crucified for his faith in Christ, he pleaded to be crucified upside down as he did not feel worthy to be executed in the same manner as his Lord and Savior. The picture of Jesus on the cross is not a piece of art, it was not as 'tame' as the painter would have you believe, in truth it was an extremely diabolical and gruesome way to die. Yet at every moment along the way, the only thought on Jesus' mind was His love for you and me. He could have come down off the cross at any time; He could have called legions of angels from heaven; He could have annihilated all of mankind at that point; but He chose to demonstrate His love and save mankind through His death as only He could. If Jesus was willing to be crucified for us, it then begs the question, *"What are we willing to do for Him?"*

Food for Thought

Have I crucified the old man or am I still living to him? How can I live victoriously over the 'old man'? – Eph. 4:22-24.

_____

_____

_____

_____

_____

_____

_____

_____

_____

_____

_____

The crucifixion was historically one of the worst forms of torture and death. Jesus was willing to not only endure the physical pain and abuse, but endured emotional and spiritual torment as well- all for me! With this in mind, what am I willing to endure for Him? It's easy to say I'd be willing to do something, so what am I doing for Him now?

_____

_____

_____

_____

_____

While I may be familiar with Christ's crucifixion from a contextual standpoint, have I ever really stopped and contemplated what Christ endured for me? If so, how can I ever live the same? What in my life needs to change?

_____

_____

_____

_____

_____

_____

_____

_____

Describe what it must have been like on the day of Christ's crucifixion. Describe the similarities and differences of then and now.

_____

_____

_____

_____

_____

_____

_____

_____

Describe all that I have obtained through Christ's death, burial and resurrection using scripture. Be specific.

_____

_____

_____

_____

_____

_____

_____

_____

_____

_____

✝

Week 9
SUNBATHING

When Jesus saw him and knew he had been ill for a long time, he asked him, "Would you like to get well?" "I can't, sir," the sick man said, "for I have no one to put me into the pool when the water bubbles up. Someone else always gets there ahead of me." Jesus told him, "Stand up, pick up your mat, and walk!"
- John 5:6-8

Years ago a story was told about Larry Walters, a 33-year-old man who decided he wanted to see his neighborhood from a new perspective. He went down to the local army surplus store one morning and bought forty-five used weather balloons. That afternoon he strapped himself into a lawn chair, to which several of his friends tied the now helium-filled balloons. He took along a six-pack of beer, a peanut-butter-and-jelly sandwich, and a BB gun, figuring he could shoot the balloons one at a time when he was ready to land.

Walters, who assumed the balloons would lift him about 100

feet in the air, was caught off guard when the chair soared more than 11,000 feet into the sky -- smack into the middle of the air traffic pattern at Los Angeles International Airport. Too frightened to shoot any of the balloons, he stayed airborne for more than two hours, forcing the airport to shut down its runways for much of the afternoon, causing long delays in flights from across the country.

Soon after he was safely grounded and cited by the police, reporters asked him three questions:

"Where you scared?" "Yes."
"Would you do it again?" "No."
"Why did you do it?" "Because," he said, *"you can't just sit there."*

The healing of the man at the pool of Bethesda is a story with many lessons for us to learn – from the need for companionship and support to the inability to thwart the masses to the need for faith and action in order to see what God can do in one's life. According to the Bible there was a tradition that an angel moved the waters at certain times and healed the sick. The issue for the man in question was that he had been laying by the pool for 38 years and because he had no one to help him into the pool once the healing touch occurred, he was left paralyzed as others would immediately beat him to the pool.

As Jesus approached He was immediately drawn to this man. (A side lesson that we can again see from Christ is that He did not wait for the sick and sinful to come to Him but He went to them; oftentimes having to intentionally go out of

His way.) However, back to the story. As Jesus approached this particular man He asked him a question that, at face value, must have seemed ridiculous, *"Would you like to get well?"* This man, who once again had been by the side of the pool for 38 years, must have thought to himself, 'Why else would I be here?' However, instead of criticizing Christ's question or answering sarcastically, this man simply responded with what was a truthful answer, yet at the same time, may have been seen as an excuse, self-pity or complaining. *"I can't, sir,"* the sick man said, *"for I have no one to put me into the pool when the water bubbles up. Someone else always gets there ahead of me."* This man was poor, sick and alone on so many levels.

As was Jesus' custom, He simply walked over to the man, stretched out His hand and said, *"Stand up, pick up your mat, and walk!"* Immediately the man was healed! The Bible does not tell us if Jesus required any action from this man as He did when His servant Elisha told Naaman to, *"Go and wash yourself seven times in the Jordan River. Then your skin will be restored, and you will be healed of your leprosy"* - 2 Kings 5:10 or if the man was healed by faith as was the woman with a blood disorder who, *"Coming up behind Jesus, she touched the fringe of his robe. Immediately, the bleeding stopped."* - Luke 8:44. This man may have simply been one of the many that Jesus healed out of His extreme love and compassion and as an example to show those following Him that He was, and is, God incarnate. Regardless, one lesson that we can learn and apply today is that God requires faith and action on our behalf if He is to work mightily in our lives.

All too often we desire to be the person like the man by the pool, simply in the right place at the right time, instead of exhibiting faith and action in what God chooses to do through our lives. James 2:17 instructs us, "...*faith by itself isn't enough. Unless it produces good deeds, it is dead and useless.*" Over and over during Jesus' ministry and in the miraculous healings he demonstrated, we see not only faith but action. For instance, in Matthew 9:27-31 we read about two blind men who approached Jesus, demonstrating action and faith through calling out to Him for healing; verbally acknowledging their faith in Him and then demonstrated in action.

It is time that we stop laying around as invalids waiting for just the right moment when Jesus will walk by and touch us. Too many days and years of our lives are wasted through the inability to act on our faith. If God has given us faith, then it's incumbent on us to put it into works. At the same time, we are instructed as we, "*Take delight in the LORD, and he will give you your heart's desires.*" - Psalm 37:4. So as we have been given godly desires, are we willing to act upon them? Jesus told us in Matthew 7:7-8, "*Keep on asking, and you will receive what you ask for. Keep on seeking, and you will find. Keep on knocking, and the door will be opened to you. For everyone who asks, receives. Everyone who seeks, finds. And to everyone who knocks, the door will be opened*", demonstrating the need for action as much as the foundation of faith.

Steve Maraboli once said, "*Faith is the poetry of our dreams; Action is the builder of our reality.*" Today, let us begin putting our faith into action and witnessing what great things God is longing to do in and through our lives. Will you continue to lay by the pool or will you get into it?

Food for Thought

Do I believe in the healing, cleansing power of the 'pool'? If so, why am I just laying here? What can I do to get into the pool? Do I need assistance?

_____

_____

_____

_____

_____

_____

It's time I stopped tanning poolside and dove in. The Christian life is meant to be mobilized not stationary. Describe what can I do today to go all in with my Christian walk?

_____

_____

_____

_____

_____

_____

This paralyzed man needed support for action in life. Do I have those in my life that I can count on to help in times of need or am I doing life alone? How can I circle up with those who will strengthen my Christian resolve?

_____

_____

_____

_____

_____

The old adage says, *"Actions speak louder than words."* How can I demonstrate to others I truly believe what I say through action?

_____

_____

_____

_____

Am I, as Jesus, seeking out those in need and attempting to demonstrate Christ's love and healing power? How? If not, why?

_____

_____

_____

_____

_____

✝

Week 10
BODY OF WORK

And I saw a great white throne and the one sitting on it. The earth and sky fled from his presence, but they found no place to hide. I saw the dead, both great and small, standing before God's throne. And the books were opened, including the Book of Life. And the dead were judged according to what they had done, as recorded in the books. The sea gave up its dead, and death and the grave gave up their dead. And all were judged according to their deeds. Then death and the grave were thrown into the lake of fire. This lake of fire is the second death. And anyone whose name was not found recorded in the Book of Life was thrown into the lake of fire.
- Revelation 20:11-15

The story is told how in a log cabin, deep within the woods, after the Battle of Bull Run, General Barnard Bee lay dying. The only words he could muster were, *"Find Imboden! Find Imboden!"* Apparently, John D. Imboden, a Virginia lawyer turned State legislator, who would command an irregular cavalry force, blamed and cursed Bee for leaving him and his men unsupported. When the dying General learned of this, he so desired to explain to Imboden with his own lips that he had given orders for his relief. As the night dragged on, the men scouted the fields and the woods, trudging up and down every country road, searching for missing Imboden. Finally, they found him and brought him to the cabin where Bee was dying. Completely broken by regret and remorse, that he had so misunderstood the directives of his commanding officer, Imboden took Bee by the hand and called him by name. No anger now; he simply spoke softly, respectfully and affectionately; however, there was no answer! He had arrived too late as the dying General was unable to share his explanation! It was also too late now for Imboden, who would become a prominent figure in the war between brothers, the Civil War, to take back his reckless and mistaken accusations.

How much of life and the actions we've committed will we regret, sorrow over and beg forgiveness for on that day where we stand before the Almighty, Righteous Judge and yet it will be too late. There will be a judgment for all. Whether we be found in Christ with our lives hid in Him and our sins forgiven or whether one stands before Christ to be judged for all the sins of their life, there is no escaping this coming day. The Bible is clear that in the end the only thing that will matter is whether our name is recorded in the Lamb's Book of Life.

Life is fast and life is short. President Lincoln once said, *"In the end, it's not the years in your life that count. It's the life in your years."* Likewise, in the same vein, Martin Luther King,

Jr. noted, *"The quality not the longevity of one's life is what is important."* Many of us today spend so much time, effort and money on trying to hold back the years; attempting to sidestep age, wrinkles and ultimately death. Instead, our time would be better spent preparing for eternity by investing into our relationship with God and others. Consider this – at the end of life, at the final judgment, would one be comfortable with his life playing out on the universal big screen for all to see, (every deed both good and bad) or would we desire when asked about our life to simply respond, Jesus is enough.

From the beginning of time man has thought himself to be capable of working his way into heaven; he has thought that if his good deeds outweighed his wrong, that he would be found worthy of everlasting life; and some have gone as far as to believe that if they perform even heinous acts in the name of God, that God will eventually reward them for such diabolical exploits. However, the Bible teaches in Isaiah 64:6, *"We are all infected and impure with sin. When we display our righteous deeds, they are nothing but filthy rags. Like autumn leaves, we wither and fall, and our sins sweep us away like the wind."* Likewise, Paul wrote in Ephesians 2:8-9 teaching, *"God saved you by his grace when you believed. And you can't take credit for this; it is a gift from God. Salvation is not a reward for the good things we have done, so none of us can boast about it."* In the end, on that day, the only work that will matter is the work of Christ on Calvary and in our hearts.

There is a story that so vividly illustrates the work that Christ has done for us, the trust we must place in His work and the saving grace that will thus spare us. In the days of the pioneers, a group was making their way across one of the central states to a distant place that had been opened up for homesteading. They traveled in covered wagons drawn by oxen and progress was extremely slow. One day they were horrified to note a long line of smoke in the west, stretching for miles across the prairie, and soon it was evident that the dried grass was burning fiercely and coming toward them rapidly. They had crossed a river the day before but it would be impossible to go back to that before the flames would be upon them. Only one man seemed to have understanding as to what could be done. He gave the command to set fire to the grass behind them. Then when a space was burned over, the whole company moved back upon it.

As the flames roared on toward them from the west, a little girl cried out in terror, *"Are you sure we shall not all be burned up?"* The leader replied, *"My child, the flames cannot reach us here, for we are standing where the fire has been!"* Christ has burned that ground for us when he took on the flames of hell and as long as we are willing to step into the safe space He created, He will also deliver us from the flames of hell.

Every person desires to look back on his life and to believe that he made a difference; that the collective works of his life somehow bettered life for all; and much like the character of George Bailey, in It's a Wonderful Life, know that it mattered that they lived. However, the true test of a man's life and his body of work will be revealed on that day when Christ either says, *"'Well done, good and faithful servant! Let's celebrate together!"*

- Matthew 25:21 or whether He says, *"I never knew you. Get away from me, you who break God's laws."* - Matthew 7:23. May our soul be hid in the crucified body of the risen Savior!

Food for Thought

At this point in my life, what do my works say about me? About my Savior? And about what's important in life?

_____

_____

_____

_____

_____

_____

_____

What am I investing my life in? Possessions or Relationships? Temporal or Eternal? How do I know? Would God agree?

_____

_____

_____

_____

_____

_____

_____

Since I don't know what chapter my life is, what can I do now to ensure a 'happy ending' in the final chapter?

_____

_____

_____

_____

_____

Just like George Bailey learned that his life did make a difference to so many, think about who has impacted my life and, if possible, let them know. We never know how long we have or how long we will have others. What would I like others to comment about my life at my funeral? What do I think they'd actually say? If I had to write my obituary, what would it say?

_____

_____

_____

_____

_____

_____

_____

_____

_____

At the end of life, we will either be judged at the Bema Seat from the Lamb's Book of Life or the Judgment Seat of Christ for our sins. Where will my judgement occur? Why? Even if at the Bema Seat, will the recap of my life be all it could've been? What can I change or do differently today?

_____

_____

_____

_____

_____

_____

_____

_____

_____

_____

_____

✝

Week 11
I DIDN'T THINK
YOU'D BE HERE

Look beneath the surface so you can judge correctly.
- John 7:24

John Hannah once remarked, *"Two things will surprise us when we arrive in heaven: who is there and who is not."* A humorous anecdote relates the way we often perceive who will be and who will not be in Heaven. The narrative goes on to say, *"A man arrived at the gates of heaven. St. Peter asked him, "Religion?"*

The man replied, *"Methodist."*

St. Peter looked down at his list and said, *"Go to Room 24, but be very quiet as you pass Room 8."*

Another man arrived at the gates of heaven. *"Religion?"*

"Lutheran."

"Go to Room 18, but be very quiet as you pass Room 8."

A third man arrived at the gates. *"Religion?"*

"Presbyterian."

"Go to Room 11, but be very quiet as you pass Room 8."

The man said, *"I can understand there being different rooms for different denominations, but why must I be quiet when I pass Room 8?"*

St. Peter replied, *"Well, the Baptists are in Room 8, and they think they're the only ones here."*

While we know that religion in and of it-self doesn't save anyone, it also doesn't disqualify anyone. Many believers race through life speculating that they will be the only ones in heaven and look down upon others thinking, 'There's no way they'll be in heaven', but how many on that day, will be surprised, even flabbergasted, to see us enter through the gates to meet our Savior?

For many it's easy to judge, intentionally or not, the salvation of another. We base our decisions on what type of music one listens to, the length of a woman's dress, whether a man wears a tie and jacket to church, if one watches television, allows their child to trick or treat, what version of the Bible one uses, whether one consumes alcohol and the list of man's requirements go on and on; all the time forgetting that our own logic, theology and judgment are erroneous. In fact, Jesus said in Luke 6:41-43 regarding judging another, *"And why worry about a speck in your friend's eye when you have a log in your own? How can you think of saying, 'Friend, let me help you get rid of that speck in your eye,' when you can't see past the log in your own eye? Hypocrite! First get rid of the log in your own eye; then you will see well enough to deal with the speck in your friend's eye."* While it is important to have standards, we must remember the only real standard is the Word of God.

Additionally, it's important we keep in mind that we are all at different places with respect to our spiritual journey or sanctification. We all come to Jesus the same way, by way of the cross and His sacrifice. But we all need to remember that, just as children learn at different paces, we also learn and grow at different rates. Even more so, we should not be conjecturing on one's eternal destiny by our own standards of what a Christian ought to be. Let us not forget how Jesus told the story of those who appeared to have it all together and yet when it came down to the finish, it was said of them, *"Not everyone who calls out to me, 'Lord! Lord!' will enter the Kingdom of Heaven. Only those who actually do the will of my Father in heaven will enter. On judgment day many will say to me, 'Lord! Lord! We prophesied in your name and cast out demons in your name and performed many miracles in your name.' But I will reply, 'I never knew you. Get away from me, you who break God's laws.'"* - Matthew 7:21-23.

Whether it be one local body deciding not to partner and fellowship with another local body of believers or an individual believer who decides to alienate himself from another over a personal preference, the more we allow the enemy to divide us, the easier it is for him to overcome us. We need to stand for truth and to stand on truth but we need not to cut another down because he doesn't dress the way we do or worship the way we choose. The Church has gone from being a hospital for the sick to a 'physician sponsored suicide' department where we put down our own instead of ministering healing to their ills. We are reminded that our common foe is Satan not each other. Let us stop critiquing one another and hold fast to the exhortation of Paul in Romans 14: 1, *"Accept other believers who are weak in faith, and don't argue with them about what they think is right or wrong."*

One day we will all stand before the Righteous Judge who will examine every man whether he be in Him or not; until then let us look to encourage fellow believers, witness to the unbelieving and realize that if it wasn't but for the grace of God, it's a certainty we would not grace the courts of heaven either. If today was to be our Home Going, would those there to receive us be surprised? If so, let us change today the way we live.

Food for Thought

Do I judge others based upon my relationship with God? What about my understanding of the Gospel or Scripture makes me believe I cannot or should not fellowship with believers of other denominations? How can I change to ensure I show the love of Christ to all fellow believers?

_____

_____

_____

_____

_____

_____

_____

Jesus said, *"When you did it to one of the least of these my brothers and sisters, you were doing it to me!"* - Matthew 25:40 . What can I do to foster a greater unity among the Saints here on earth so that the world may see the love of Christ?

_____

_____

_____

_____

_____

_____

_____

While we know that religion doesn't save anyone, we also know the Word says, *"Pure and genuine religion in the sight of God the Father means caring for orphans and widows in their distress and refusing to let the world corrupt you."* - James 1:27. Am I being corrupted by man-made religious rules (referred to as legalism) or is my relationship with Christ growing stronger every day? Why or why not?

_____

_____

_____

_____

_____

_____

_____

May I always remember on this journey called life, there will be those ahead of me and those behind me but all that matters is that I keep moving forward following Christ.

Week 12
INFILTRATED BY THE ENEMY

Even that question came up only because of some so-called believers there—false ones, really— who were secretly brought in. They sneaked in to spy on us and take away the freedom we have in Christ Jesus. They wanted to enslave us and force us to follow their Jewish regulations
- Galatians 2:4

What must it be like to have to leave your home, your friends, your family, everything you've ever known to travel by foot hundreds, possibly thousands of miles without food, water, provisions of any kind just in hopes of saving your life? Enemy infiltration often causes a population displacement simply because for the people involved it's either flee or fight and most are not equipped to fight. Today, and for months now, many have been fleeing Syria. ISIS continues to take a strangle hold on the land through subjecting Syrians to murder, torture, crucifixion, sexual slavery, among other atrocities. In addition, Syrian's President, Bashar al-Assad continues to target his citizens with chemical weapons and barrel bombs. The estimate today is that 4.1 million Syrians are fleeing their country after multiple years of civil war. Of this number, it is believed that more than half are under the age of seventeen. As one would expect, this massive exodus of people is more than any one country can absorb because of economic hardship upon the contributing countries and the likelihood that not everyone is a legitimate refugee. To be real, when dealing with such an extreme magnitude of people there may well be enemy infiltration within the ranks.

These are real life actions and decisions that need to be made when dealing with the 'collateral damage' of ruthless dictators and ideologies that are determined to eradicate whatever and whoever in order to establish their own beliefs. Enemy infiltration has always been a strategic maneuver used to kill and destroy the innocent, those willing to lend a helping hand or simply those who are oblivious to the danger around them. When one is able to assimilate into the larger group without fear of being recognized or discovered, it is then that they gain the upper hand to execute their plans of destruction; whether the plans be philosophical or pragmatic.

Digging deeper and being transparent, have you ever considered how our spiritual enemy infiltrates our lives on a daily basis to bring destruction? All the way back to Genesis 3 we read of the enemy's subtle yet destructive approach. In verses 1-5 we read, *to "The serpent was the shrewdest of all the wild animals the Lord God had made. One day he asked the woman, "Did God really say you must not eat the fruit from any of the trees in the garden?" "Of* course we may eat fruit from the trees in the garden," the woman replied. "It's only the fruit from the tree in the middle of the garden that we are not allowed to eat. God said, 'You must not eat it or even touch it; if you do, you will die.'" "You won't die!" the serpent replied to the woman. "God knows that your eyes will be opened as soon as you eat it, and you will be like God, knowing both good and evil." - Genesis 3:1-5. This is an example of how the enemy used a less 'in your face' approach and yet was able to get Eve to walk down a road that has had lasting consequences for all mankind. Additionally, regarding assimilation, by those who aren't what they say they are, we are cautioned in Matthew 7:15, "Beware of false prophets who come disguised as harmless sheep but are really vicious wolves." - Matthew 7:15. This is an area where many are drawn in and risk attack. Finally, we read in I Peter 5:8 about the overt attacks of the enemy when we read, "Stay alert! Watch out for your great enemy, the devil. He prowls around like a roaring lion, looking for someone to devour." Enemy infiltration comes in many forms, at many different times and with many different consequences. It may be the most dangerous yet effective strategy an enemy combatant can use because it often takes the victim by surprise and has lasting and lethal repercussions.

While the United States has always been a humanitarian nation, today's times and our nation's enemies have backed us into a place where we need to be cautious, vigilant, and even apprehensive to allowing others into our land without the proper vetting process. While the importance of this security measure is acutely prevalent today, how much more attentiveness needs to be paid to our spiritual condition and the battle we are in every day? Remember, we are admonished in Ephesians 6 of the spiritual warfare that we are a participant in, whether that be through passive engagement or active engagement.

We are in hostile territory. There are mine fields all around us. How are we safeguarding ourselves from the infiltration of the enemy? Our families? Our churches? Our country? Jesus warned of this in Mark 7:20-22 when He noted, *"And then he added, "It is what comes from inside that defiles you. For from within, out of a person's heart, come evil thoughts, sexual immorality, theft, murder, adultery, greed, wickedness, deceit, lustful desires, envy, slander, pride and foolishness."* Beware! If we do not take a proactive battle stance to fight such evil, it will creep in slowly but surely through the act of infiltration.

Food for Thought

What areas has the enemy infiltrated my life? How can I protect my life from enemy infiltration?

_____

_____

_____

_____

_____

How does the enemy seek to use my relationships against me?

_____

_____

_____

_____

It has often been said, *"Don't settle for good when great is within reach."* Have I become preoccupied with the good and laid waste of the great? How?

_____

_____

_____

_____

It's extremely easy to become busy in ministry, does that mean I'm being effective? Could busyness in ministry be an infiltration? Why?

_____

_____

_____

_____

How can I safeguard my life so as not to allow the enemy a threshold?

_____

_____

_____

_____

_____

What must I do to be a beacon to those on the battle field; sounding the alarm about a dangerous, subtle, deadly enemy? Am I safeguarding the lives of my family, friends and community? If so, how? If not, what can I do?

_____

_____

_____

_____

_____

✝

Week 13

GET OUT OF
THE BOAT

Yes, come," Jesus said. So Peter went over the side of
the boat and walked on the water toward Jesus.
- Matthew 14:29

As someone who grew up enjoying salt-water activities all summer, from fishing to clamming to water skiing, the thought of getting out of the boat into deep, cold waters seems a bit extreme. Think about it - it's one thing to get into water where you can feel the bottom or even into warm water to swim around, but to get out of a boat during a horrific storm, when the boat is the only thing between you and a tragic death, seems illogical and insane. Yet that is exactly what Peter was willing to do when Jesus called to him, *"Come"*.

I have heard many lessons over the years about Peter getting out of the boat and walking on water to Jesus but most of the times it has been focused on Peter taking his eyes off of Jesus and thus sinking. While this is true, would any of us have done any different? For howling winds, driving rain in one's face, sky-illuminating lightning strikes and crashing booms of thunder would be enough to distract anyone. It's very easy to sit here today and say, *"If only Peter had kept his eyes on Jesus."* But then we must ask ourselves, Do we?

Anyone can see the obvious, eyes on Jesus equals peace in the storm; while eyes off of Jesus, focusing on the distractions and noise of life, will equal sinking into the pit of a cold and perilous grave. However, we scarcely consider the intestinal fortitude, 'guts', that it took for Peter to get out of the boat in the first place knowing what was taking place around him. Additionally, he was the ONLY one that had the faith to do so. Where were all of the other disciples when Peter got out of the boat? Why did they not join him? They had all witnessed Jesus' miracles and professed they believed in Him as God's Son. Did they actually believe Peter was crazy and did they try to prevent him from getting into the water? For at that time they had no idea he would be able to walk on the water. How many of them later regretted missing out on such a miracle? So many questions that we will never have answers to, on this side of heaven but one thing is for sure, we need to have the faith and courage to get out of our boats and begin walking toward Jesus.

For many today we have become paralyzed in our fear, anxiety, circumstances, disbelief and so many other negative feelings that we are content to crawl to the front of the boat and hide under the bow instead of taking Christ at His word and walking on water. Yes, the winds are ever so loud. The rain is so driving we can hardly see. The lightning is ridiculous! The thunder booms as if the whole world will explode. But do we see and hear it or are we so consumed with Christ and our faith in Him that it all just drowns into the background?

Many people say they want to do mighty works; they want to change the world but how can that be done if they're hiding from every difficulty they encounter? Peter did a lot of things wrong but very few have had the courage to do what He did. How many others do you know where it was ever recorded that they walked on water? Even if it was but just for a moment!

How exciting must it have been to do something that defied all natural occurrences?! Today we follow and serve the same Christ that allowed Peter to walk on water. So, what is holding you back? What is preventing you from walking on water? What is causing you to take your eyes off the One who walked on water? Yes, the boat is comfortable; it's warm; and it keeps us 'safe'. Or is the boat keeping us from stepping out and doing something miraculous? We've seen what life looks like inside the boat, how about getting outside of it and seeing what life is like on the waters?

Food for Thought

How am I responding to the storm around me? Hunkered down in the cabin crying or bravely looking unto Christ for rescue? What actions in my life signify this?

_____

_____

_____

_____

_____

_____

Do I hear Jesus' voice over the roar of the sea and the mighty winds? What is He saying to me? Am I listening? Am I obeying?

_____

_____

_____

_____

_____

_____

Have I at other times sank in the deep waters, thus making me nervous to try again? What can I do to overcome this fear and be used of God again?

_____

_____

_____

_____

_____

Do I trust Jesus enough to get out of the boat and begin walking toward Him? What am I doing that validates this trust?

_____

_____

_____

_____

_____

Will I be remembered for trusting Jesus enough to get out the boat onto the rough seas to follow Him or will I be characterized by fear and doubt and remain in the boat? Why?

_____

_____

_____

_____

_____

Week 14
IT'S TIME THE CHURCH GOT ANGRY

But God shows his anger from heaven against all sinful, wicked people who suppress the truth by their wickedness. They know the truth about God because he has made it obvious to them.
- Romans 1:18-19

Long gone are the days of preachers like Billy Sunday, D.L. Moody, Charles Spurgeon and many more who would make no apologies for preaching the word of God with passion and conviction, praying the Holy Spirit would grip the hearts of their congregates and drive them to their knees in repentance. Sermons that would cast the light of the gospel upon the sin and darkness of this world. Sermons that would cause the believer to access their relationship with God and their motives for sharing the truth of the Word. Sermons that would take up the battle cry and send warriors of the cross into the field to wage war against immorality, drunkenness, lying and deceit, apathy and so many more. Preachers of years gone by would agonize in their spirit as to the present day moral condition of our country. And they would not sit back and believe they could not change the spiritual atmosphere or express righteous anger over the vomitus sin and eternal indifference of the saints of God.

Billy Sunday was often quoted making statements such as, *"A revival does two things. First, it returns the Church from her backsliding and second, it causes the conversion of men and women; and it always includes the conviction of sin on the part of the Church. What a spell the devil seems to cast over the Church today!"* Likewise, he said, *"The rivers of America will run with blood filled to their banks before we will submit to them taking the Bible out of our schools"* and *"I have been, and will go on, fighting that damnable, dirty, rotten business with all the power at my command."*

Additionally, D.L. Moody was known for quotes such as, *"The Bible will keep you from sin, or sin will keep you from the Bible"* and *"We are told to let our light shine, and if it does, we won't need to tell anybody it does. Lighthouses don't fire cannons to call attention to their shining – they just shine."* Then there is Charles Spurgeon who would expound truths like, *"We have come to a turning point in the road. If we turn to the right mayhap our children and our children's children will go that way; but if we turn to the left, generations yet unborn will curse our names for having been unfaithful to God and to His Word"*. Even more he went on to say, *"Cast away your sloth, your lethargy, your coldness, or whatever interferes with your chaste and pure love for Christ, your soul's husband. Make Him the source, the center and the circumference of all your soul's range of delight."*

Does this sound like the weak, shaking words of frail men concerned with political correctness, diversity and inclusion? Or, are these the words of valiant soldiers of the cross who understood what was at stake, and because of their fervent desire to preach Christ and save sinners from hell, where willing to share the truth at the expense of large congregations or social nobility?

Today's Church is in need of such men that are willing to stand and cry, *"Thus says the Lord...get your life right!"* Even more, we need those who are less concerned with the acceptance of man and more focused on the words of *"Well done, my good and faithful servant"*. It is impossible for man to please the world and God. The question thus exists, when will we say enough is enough?

We have been fooled and lulled into believing that as Christians we do not have the right to express righteous anger over sin. The Church has been sold a false bill of goods that too many have come to buy that standing against immorality is some way discriminatory. Even further, too many of the younger generation have come to believe that God is simply a God of love to the detriment of leaving out holiness and righteousness.

So many issues that seem to be acceptable in mainstream America would never have come to light if the Church had done her job. For whatever reason the Church has decided to take a 'time-out' and let the world go on as if we have no responsibility for its course. The complete decay of our moral fabric seems to reach a new low everyday. And when, even the world, begins to wonder where the outcry is against such debauchery, all the Church seems to do is sit back in the fetal position acting as if it makes no difference. Is this what Jesus would do? Is this what Jesus did do? The answer is a resounding -NO!

In fact, when Jesus approached the temple and found so many selling and profiting from those desiring to worship God, did He just turn around and walk away, murmuring, *"It doesn't affect me so why should I care."* Once again, *"NO!"* Jesus exhibited righteous indignation! He turned the tables of the money collectors over, he made a whip and began to scourge and chase these ungodly ones from the temple and He recognized His role in the situation. He expressed a righteous anger for the things of His Father. He realized and rebuked those who attempted to make a mockery of the things of God. He did not just choose to ignore it.

Where is the righteous anger from the Church today? Does Christ care any less about the sin and depravity in today's world? Why as Christians do we feel that we have no responsibility in the social issues of our day, which are really biblical issues? If God has declared it sin, who is man to say otherwise? How is it that sin doesn't make our blood boil? I'll tell you why - because we are the frog in the pot of water. Frog you ask. Yes. We are the frog in the pot of water that has felt the temperature increase slowly but because we simply adjusted to it we did not see the horrible end it would eventually bring. If on the other hand, we would have been thrown into a boiling pot of water, we would have immediately jumped out realizing the deadly consequences.

Let me encourage you brothers and sisters, it is NOT too late. The hour is late and the skies are dark but there is still hope. As long as the Lord tarries it is His expectation we be busy about His work. We are not to give up on those around us, on our country and certainly not on our families. We must be about calling out sin and not accepting the immoral overreaches of government policies. It is time for the Church to get angry! Be willing to be the voice that starts the domino effect because of personal revival, and then share it with someone else; anyone, everyone. Time is short and our backs are against the wall but that is when true warriors show what they are made of and we are made of Christ!

Food for Thought

What is the difference between selfish anger and Christ's righteous indignation?

_____

_____

_____

_____

_____

What makes me angry? How do I respond?

_____

_____

_____

_____

_____

How should I act toward sin? Can I be upset with sin and yet
not sin myself?

_____

_____

_____

_____

_____

Have I bought into the lie 'sin is not sin'? How do I know? Do
I now accept 'small' sins or sins 'that don't affect me'? What do
I need to do to change?

_____

_____

_____

_____

_____

_____

Do I hate the sin but love the sinner? Does the sinner agree?

_____

_____

_____

_____

_____

As believers we are to be the light and salt of the world. What can I do to shine a light upon and oppose sin around me? In my family? In my church? In my country?

_____

_____

_____

_____

_____

_____

_____

_____

_____

_____

Week 15
GIVE US OUR DAILY BREAD

And this same God who takes care of me will supply all your needs from his glorious riches, which have been given to us in Christ Jesus.
- Philippians 4:19

Life can be full of uncertainty, it can be extremely anxious and there are many times it is filled with doubt, fear and apprehension. Life is no different today than any other time in history to the extent that we often wonder, 'how am I going to pay my bills?', 'how am I going to put gas in my car?', how am I going to put food on my table, new shoes on my kids' feet or provide for my family's medical coverage?' If one thinks that these fears and concerns don't exist in America or perhaps you don't happen to actually know of anyone struggling with these issues, just look around. They may actually be closer than you think.

Chuck Swindoll once asserted, *"The matters we or the world might consider trivial, He cares about and wants to remedy. He longs to relieve our worries and has promised to supply our most fundamental needs.*" Furthermore, Jesus exhorted us in Matthew 6:25-32, "*That is why I tell you not to worry about everyday life—whether you have enough food and drink, or enough clothes to wear. Isn't life more than food, and your body more than clothing? Look at the birds. They don't plant or harvest or store food in barns, for your heavenly Father feeds them. And aren't you far more valuable to him than they are? Can all your worries add a single moment to your life?*" "*And why worry about your clothing? Look at the lilies of the field and how they grow. They don't work or make their clothing, yet Solomon in all his glory was not dressed as beautifully as they are. And if God cares so wonderfully for wildflowers that are here today and thrown into the fire tomorrow, he will certainly care for you. Why do you have so little faith?*" "*So don't worry about these things, saying, 'What will we eat? What will we drink? What will we wear?' These things dominate the thoughts of unbelievers, but your heavenly Father already knows all your needs.*"

As believers we should absolutely respond in a much more positive manner. We should not worry. We should not fear. We should not try to figure it all out on our own or presume we can actually take care of ourselves. While it is only human nature, we need to remember if we are in Christ then we are so much more than physical. Where we often falter is in our disbelief that God will provide. We talk a good game but we fail to actually implement it. When we hear of missionary experiences or stories of old we think, 'well that was then and that was great how God came through but my situation is so different...it's so much larger' and because of our disbelief we not only prevent God from showing up and showing off in our lives but we also sin against God in the process.

A very real example of the way that God meets our daily needs, even before we know they exist, is told in a story about an orphanage that George Mueller operated in the 1800's.

"The children are dressed and ready for school. But there is no food for them to eat," the housemother of the orphanage informed George Mueller. George asked her to take the 300 children into the dining room and have them sit at the tables. He thanked God for the food and waited. George knew God would provide food for the children as he always did. Within minutes, a baker knocked on the door. *"Mr. Mueller,"* he said, *"last night I could not sleep. Somehow I knew that you would need bread this morning. I got up and baked three batches for you. I will bring it in."* Soon, there was another knock at the door. It was the milkman. His cart had broken down in front of the orphanage. The milk would spoil by the time the wheel was fixed. He asked George if he could use some free milk. George smiled as the milkman brought in ten large cans of milk. It was just enough for the 300 thirsty children.

Instances like this we would call miracles. We would also many times chalk it up to past events that no longer take place today. However, I would argue the difference being we don't pray and believe that God will provide and we especially don't believe He will provide in such an abnormal, theatrical way. But why not? He is still the same God of the Bible, the same God that provided the bread and milk for Mr. Mueller's orphanage and the same God that desires to meet our needs today. The Bible exhorts us in Philippians 4:6-7, *"Don't worry about anything; instead, pray about everything. Tell God what you need, and thank him for all he has done. Then you will experience God's peace, which exceeds anything we can understand. His peace will guard your hearts and minds as you live in Christ Jesus."*

Today, let us begin to believe and practice faith in God's provision for us. He has not brought you to leave you. He has not brought you to something that He will not bring you through. While we cannot always see the way our prayers will be answered and our needs met, that is not our concern. We are simply instructed to let God know of our needs and then to trust Him and watch what He does. He will never disappoint and we will stand amazed at the abundance He will bring into our lives.

Food for Thought

Do I really know the difference between a need and a want? What need has God provided today? Take a moment and thank Him for it.

_____

_____

_____

_____

_____

_____

Describe a time where I forewent a personal need in order to meet someone else's need. If I haven't, determine who and how I can meet a need. Note: Put love into action.

_____

_____

_____

_____

_____

_____

Am I more concerned with tomorrow than today? What can I do to stop worrying about future needs and grow my faith?

_____

_____

_____

_____

_____

_____

_____

_____

Is my prayer/faith life focused on communion and praise of God or on treating Him like a wish list? Does my prayer/faith life focus on needs or wants? How can I make sure I am asking for my 'daily bread'? Am I thanking Him for meeting my daily needs?

_____

_____

_____

_____

_____

_____

If my meal depended upon my prayer/faith life, would I be eating a turkey or a pigeon? If I don't like pigeon, how do I need to change my prayer/faith life?

_____

_____

_____

_____

_____

_____

✝

Week 16
IT'LL ONLY HURT FOR
A FEW MINUTES

The bloodthirsty hate blameless people,
but the upright seek to help them.
- Proverbs 29:10

I recently heard a story about a Pastor in Iraq that was desperately racing from house to house of his parishioners warning them to leave town as fast as they could as ISIS was quickly approaching. As he could hear the sound of gunfire getting ever so closer, he realized he would soon run out of time. Quickly and frantically rushing to the house of a family that held an extra special place in his heart, he knew there was no longer enough time to run. As he reached the house and the door opened, he urgently warned the family that momentarily ISIS would be upon them. They would then be asked if they were Christians and upon their answer death would be the payment. As you can imagine these poor people were fearful but as the pastor reminded them, *"It'll only hurt for a few moments."* Their response was *"How can we deny Jesus?"* With the thought and reality of eminent torture and ultimate death literally at their doorstep, this family's response was not 'Why'. Instead the only thought that existed in their minds and hearts was their desire to give their lives for their Lord and Savior, Jesus Christ. What faith! What devotion! Martin Luther King, Jr. understood something about this when he wrote, *"The ultimate measure of a man is not where he stands in moments of comfort and convenience, but where he stands at times of challenge and controversy."*

Today, in the United States, we do not fear such retribution for our faith, yet for some reason Christians find it difficult to take biblical stands for what is right. We are instructed in Romans 12:1-2 as such *"And so, dear brothers and sisters, I plead with you to give your bodies to God because of all he has done for you. Let them be a **living and holy sacrifice**—the kind he will find acceptable. This is truly the way to worship him. Don't copy the behavior and customs of this world, but let God transform you into a new person by changing the way you think. Then you will learn to know God's will for you, which is good and pleasing and perfect."* We are admonished to live for Christ and here in the United States we get to do just that...**LIVE!** Our brothers and sisters in Christ in other parts of the world are not so fortunate. They are dying for Christ and yet are doing it gladly and we have difficulties simply living for Christ. Jim Elliot understood this principle as he penned and later would give his life when he wrote, *"He is no fool who gives what he cannot keep, to gain what he cannot lose."* So I ask you, what do our brothers and sisters know that we do not?

I propose that much like the early Church in the book of

Acts, growth took place under intense persecution but we have become soft, weak and undisciplined in our pursuit of Christ. Francis Chan noted about the pursuit of God that, *"We never grow closer to God when we just live life. It takes deliberate pursuit and attentiveness."* It is not until we desire God more than anything else that we find it an honor to die for Him, but until that may come, let us at least live for Him. To this measure Martin Luther wrote, *"Faith is a living and unshakable confidence; a belief in God so assured that a man would die a thousand deaths for its sake."*

As much as anyone of us may feel for fellow believers in other parts of the world and would like to believe we would be able to do the same, it may be a reach to think we would be able to die for our faith when we have a hard time living for it. Don't wait till someone shows up at your door to persecute you for your faith. Don't let others wonder where you stand. There is an old saying that goes, *"If you were to be tried in court for being a Christian, would there be enough evidence to convict you?"* Well ...would there? If so, Great! Hold the faith and keep fighting. If not, then start doing something while there is still time.

Food for Thought

While I may dare utter the words that I would be willing to die for Christ, how would I feel if truly faced with such a possibility?

_____

_____

_____

_____

_____

How do my daily actions demonstrate my faith in and allegiance to Christ?

_____

_____

_____

_____

_____

If Christ tarries His return and our society continues to devolve, we may very well have to endure persecution for Christ. How am I preparing my faith for that possibility now?

_____

_____

_____

_____

_____

Does my faith life reflect one that is so in love with Christ that there is not a smidge of myself present? If not, what needs to change? Answer honestly.

_____

_____

_____

_____

_____

Do I believe as Paul when he said, *"For to me, living means living for Christ, and dying is even better."* - Philippians 1:21. Does my life model this scripture? How? If not, what needs to change?

_____

_____

_____

_____

_____

If tried in court for being a Christian, would there be enough evidence to convict me? List the evidence.

_____

_____

_____

_____

_____

✝

Week 17
18 INCHES OF SEPARATION

The father instantly cried out, "I do believe,
but help me overcome my unbelief!
- Mark 9:24

The distance between the brain and the heart may only be 18 inches but it is often the distance between Heaven and Hell. One can know about Jesus without actually knowing Jesus. In fact, Jonathan Edwards described it this way in his sermon, Divine and Supernatural Light when he preached, *"your mind can know honey is sweet, people can tell you it's sweet, you've read books about it, etc. but if you haven't actually tasted it, you know with your head, but not with your heart. When you actually taste it, you experience it for yourself, you know it in a full way, and you can know it in your heart."*

Many a person knows about Jesus. They know we celebrate His birth on Christmas. They know of what the Bible teaches about Him. They even know that Good Friday is when He was crucified and that He arose again on Easter Sunday. They know that He is God's Son and they know He created all there is. But do they know Him through another's relationship or do they know Him personally? Do you? Do I?

Having a relationship with Christ is much more than doing good deeds, attending church on Sunday or being able to recite scripture. A true relationship is knowing the heart of someone and having them know ours. While there is no doubt God knows our heart, in order for us to know His we must spend time with Him. Imagine what a relationship would look like where neither party spent any time with the other. In time the relationship would dissolve and fade away. A relationship needs communication, quantity and quality time and a desire to spend time with each other.

Many people claim to know Christ but do they really know Him? Do they know who He is intellectually or do they know Him intimately? One's eternal stake and destiny is pent up in that one question. For one who knows Him intellectually will one day stand before Him to hear Him say, *"Not everyone who calls out to me, 'Lord! Lord!' will enter the Kingdom of Heaven. Only those who actually do the will of my Father in heaven will enter. On judgment day many will say to me, 'Lord! Lord! We prophesied in your name and cast out demons in your name and performed many miracles in your name.' But I will reply, 'I never knew you. Get away from me, you who break God's laws'"* - Matthew 7:21-23. On the other hand, those who know Christ intimately, with a heart knowledge and relationship will have the blessing of hearing Him say, *"Then the King will say to those on his right, 'Come, you who are blessed by my Father, inherit the Kingdom prepared for you from the creation of the world"* - Matthew 25:34.

Consider how a short distance can be the difference between fame and ruin. When the Navy's Blue Angels fly what is known as the Diamond 360, there is only 18 inches in the wingtip-to-canopy diamond formation between the first 4 aircrafts. Just the slightest maneuver can be the difference between a memorable air show of marksmanship and expertise or the untimely death of pilots and possible spectators.

The idea that missing heaven is because of major grievous acts is a misnomer. One does not have to be a heinous individual in order to miss heaven and end up in hell. Quite the opposite; there will be many more who go to hell that lived 'good' lives, knowing about God, but never making the relationship personal. It is the difference between knowing something theoretically and applying it practically.

An expression about closeness says, *"In horse shoes and hand grenades"*. While being close to one's target will score you points in those scenarios, with regard to heaven through a personal relationship with Christ another expression is applicable which says, *"Close but no cigar"*; the obvious and apparent meaning of one not winning the prize.

Today be sure you know God personally. Not just in your mind intellectually but deep down in your heart. How tragic would it be to come to the end of life, having been the one who knew the book, yet not having known its author? Get yourself a signed copy and let Him sign it on your heart.

Food for Thought

What is it about people that allows them to understand the facts of salvation but not to accept it personally?

_____

_____

_____

_____

_____

What specific scripture teaches me that I can KNOW I am saved?

_____

_____

_____

_____

What specific scripture teaches me 'once saved, always saved'?

_____

_____

_____

_____

Take a few moments to reflect on when I accepted Christ as Savior. What were the circumstances? What did God use to speak to my heart? Who did God use to present the gospel? How has my life changed? Thank Him for His saving grace.

_____

_____

_____

_____

_____

_____

_____

_____

_____

Think about having a spiritual birthday party each year to remember and rejoice.

✟

Week 18
AMBASSADORS OF
THE KING

So we are Christ's ambassadors; God is making his appeal through us. We speak for Christ when we plead, "Come back to God!"
- II Corinthians 5:20

The role of an ambassador, as a highest ranking official envoy, is to represent their native homeland while working and living in the foreign country they have been appointed. United States ambassadors are appointed by the President and confirmed by the Senate to speak on behalf of the President and his policies. An intricate role of an ambassador is to follow the policies of their leader and nation regardless if they agree with it on a personal level. While another function is to oversee the safety of travelling citizens within the foreign country. Even further, ambassadors communicate with the home country as to safety risks and whether fellow citizens should be travelling to such places. The responsibilities of an ambassador are far sweeping and diverse, but the role, power and privilege that comes along with the position, are by far greater than the requirements.

Many remember Ambassador Christopher Stevens whose life was taken from him, along with the lives of 3 others, on September 11, 2012, in Benghazi, Libya. While the specific details that led to that tragic day will more than likely never truly be known, the fact is, being an ambassador puts a target on one's back. Simply representing someone or something can be enough to cause adversity, calamity and hostility to be projected in one's direction. Being an ambassador requires faith in the cause, courage in the field and stamina for the course. For an ambassador realizes the mission reaches far beyond his or her interests.

As ambassadors of the Heavenly King we are to represent His interests on hostile, enemy soil. Just as Ambassador Stevens was given a mission, policies to enact and an endgame, so we too have been given like orders. Jesus told us in Matthew 28:18-20, *"I have been given all authority in heaven and on earth. Therefore, go and make disciples of all the nations, baptizing them in the name of the Father and the Son and the Holy Spirit. Teach these new disciples to obey all the commands I have given you."* As it is true, many ambassadors have the privilege of living affluent lifestyles, many more live in poverty-stricken nations, often being placed in turmoil and precarious positions. Being an ambassador is not meant to be a 'stepping stone' to selfish ambitions, it is meant to instead be a mouthpiece for someone and something greater.

Imagine how you would feel if the President called you into the Oval Office and said, *"I've got big plans for you. I want you to represent me and our country to ... You will have the complete power and authority of my office and our country behind you. If you need anything, all you have to do is ask."* We would be floored! We would most certainly put on our best and conduct ourselves in the highest manner, knowing what an honor and privilege had been bestowed on us. Now, think about it...as a Christian this is where we stand – only not in man's eyes, but God's.

Unfortunately, a number of believers today have allowed the poisoning of their minds; so much that they believe they have been 'stationed' to improve their own personal gain at the cost of failing to relay the message of Heaven to this foreign land. As seen by many, an ambassadorship is a prestigious position, but it is one meant to be held with a serving heart. Simply having the favor to speak on behalf of power and authority not our own should be a sobering thought. And it should help us to remember we were chosen at the request of someone greater, not to share our views, opinions or beliefs, but to represent the One who sent us.

Ambassadors are in its most basic form – spokespersons. Likewise, as ambassadors for Christ we are His representatives. As Paul sat in prison pondering his thoughts and praising God he proclaimed, *"I am in chains now, still preaching this message as God's ambassador. So pray that I will keep on speaking boldly for him, as I should."* - Eph. 6:20. If Ambassador Stevens had an opportunity to do things differently in regard to representing the United States of America, do you think he would have? If all that is said about him is true, I don't believe he would have changed a thing. So, if a man is willing to proudly stand by his convictions and so speak on behalf of his nation, even in the blatant face of death, how much more should we shout from the rooftops the glory of the Heavenly Father as His chosen diplomats? We have the privilege to represent the greatest King and country this world has ever known or will ever know.

Food for Thought

An ambassador lives in a foreign land yet speaks on behalf of his home country. With this in mind, am I living as an ambassador of Christ or a citizen of Earth? What specifically marks this behavior?

_____

_____

_____

_____

_____

As an ambassador of Christ, what should my life be about? What are my responsibilities and obligations? Does anything need to change?

_____

_____

_____

_____

_____

It's crucial that an ambassador know his orders. Our orders are found in the Bible. So, am I following my orders and if so, how am I speaking for my King? Or am I concealing His message? Why or why not? Be specific.

_____

_____

_____

_____

_____

_____

_____

Describe what an ambassador of Christ should be and compare my life to the ideal.

_____

_____

_____

_____

_____

_____

_____

✝

Week 19

STRADDLING
THE FENCE

Then Elijah stood in front of them and said,
"How much longer will you waver, hobbling
between two opinions? If the Lord is God,
follow him! But if Baal is God, then follow
him!" But the people were completely silent.
- I Kings 18:21

I don't know if the story is true or even remember where I heard it but the moral of the story is so applicable, I felt the need to share it with all. The story says that a particular man was looking to sell his house for a meager $1,500 in a poor South American country. He had found a desirable customer, but the man was extremely poor and couldn't afford to the pay the asking price. As the bargaining process came to a conclusion, the owner and buyer agreed that the house would change hands for half the original price with just one clause - the seller would retain sole ownership of just one small nail distending from just over the front door.

Years later, the seller wanted his house back, but the new owner was completely opposed to the idea. Eventually the first owner went out, found the rotting remains of a dead animal, and posted it from the single nail he still owned. Quickly the house became rottenness as the stench was completely unbearable. In no time at all, the family was forced to sell the house back to the owner of the nail.

The morale of the story being - If we leave the Devil with even one small nail in our life, he will make it the final nail in our coffin, making us an unfit dwelling for the Holy Spirit.

Many Christians talk about total commitment to Christ but very few are willing to live it. Just like in the story of Elijah and his encounter with the priests of Baal, God's people were not only hesitant, but completely paralyzed in their apathy, and thus unwilling to align with God in the face of evil, so is the Church of Christ today. Revelation 3 speaks to us of the different ages and stages of the Church through history and the compelling case could be made that we are today living in the age of Laodicea. In fact, as John watched all that would unfold he wrote about Christ saying, *"I know all the things you do, that you are neither hot nor cold. I wish that you were one or the other! But since you are like lukewarm water, neither hot nor cold, I will spit you out of my mouth! You say, 'I am rich. I have everything I want. I don't need a thing!' And you don't realize that you are wretched and miserable and poor and blind and naked."* - Revelation 3:15-17.

Today's Church is incapacitated from seeing the hand of God

flow through them, their families, their churches and their country because we have become too comfortable living in this world. We have forgotten what it means when Jesus said, *"Come out from among unbelievers, and separate yourselves from them, says the LORD"* - II Cor. 6:17. Even worse, we have lost the savor and effect that, as believers, we are commanded to exude. Leonard Ravenhill once commented, *"The early Church was married to poverty, prisons and persecutions. Today, the Church is married to prosperity, personality and popularity."* Unfortunately, many believers sit around and belly-ache as to the conditions of today's society but fail to see the gravity of falling to one's knees and crying out to God; more so, too many are unbothered by what is occurring around them let alone in their own lives.

Just as the Israelites were held hostage in their spiritual lives, not by physical restraint, but by a lethargic attitude to the Lord Almighty and an unwillingness to step out and be different, Christians today believe they can be part of the world without being influenced by it. We must then begin to ask ourselves, did it work for Lot? Above all people, Lot knew how he ought to live, yet he allowed the world to pull him in and the toll upon his family proved to be disastrous. It has often been said, *"As the family goes so goes the Church. As the Church goes so goes society"*.

The time is well upon us; our families are broken and hurting; our nation is on the brink of judgment and ruin; those who claim the name of Christ need to stop being concerned about what the world thinks and to begin caring what God says. Today's believer has adopted a false philosophy that says everyone and everything needs to be accepted so as not to appear unloving and judgmental; but aren't we in all reality being unloving when we refuse to live according to God's word, regardless of how it impacts others?

Just as Elijah asked the people, *"How much longer will you waver, hobbling between two opinions?"* so we must ask the same of ourselves. It's time to stop straddling the fence. One either needs to put both feet in the world or both feet in heaven, but he can't have it both ways. The lack of commitment by Christians has led to a world on fire. Today, those in the world are looking for a believer who is willing to sacrifice his own popularity to bring the message of truth that will forever change lives. If we're not willing to be that person, who will?

Food for Thought

What 'rotting carcass' do I still have in my life? Do I enjoy the smell of decaying flesh? If not, how and when am I going to remove it?

_____

_____

_____

_____

_____

_____

_____

Have I completely 'sold' the old dwelling or am I still holding onto pieces of it? If so, what and why?

_____

_____

_____

_____

_____

Describe specific actions or inactions of today's Church that demonstrate a lost influence and ineffective faith in today's world. How can the Church once again be the light in a dark world?

_____

_____

_____

_____

Responsibility begins at home. While I may not be able to change everyone, I can certainly influence those closest to me. What can I do today to ensure I am living out my faith in a way that leads others to faith in Christ?

_____

_____

_____

_____

What do I think the world thinks about Christians who seem no different than they? Do I appear different than the world? Is it genuine faith or just an act?

_____

_____

_____

_____

_____

_____

_____

_____

✝

Week 20
PROGRESSIVE CHRISTIANITY

And may you be completely faithful to the Lord our God. May you always obey his decrees and commands, just as you are doing today.
- I Kings 8:61

There has often been a comparison made between the Church of Laodicea found in Revelation 3 and the modern 21st century church of America. The Laodicea church was spiritually blind. Its members thought they were rich and in need of nothing, while the truth was, conformity was their downfall. Furthermore, the Laodicea church accepted everything and didn't stand for anything. God Himself described their actions and works as 'neither hot nor cold' (vs. 15). They were engulfed and entrapped in the philosophy of Moral relativism; *"the view that ethical standards, morality and positions of right or wrong are culturally based and therefore subject to a person's individual choice."* I am perplexed to understand the difference between Laodicea from present day. The *"Christian"* church of America can be likened to Lot, who thinking he could live outside the gates of Sodom unscathed by the immoral pollution inside, only later to find out he would be living inside the gates of the city at the peril of his family.

Today's cup of tea Christianity chooses to accept and believe that there are higher values than living a life of commitment to the cross, on the Bible and in the Savior. The belief that love trumps all and that loving others more will make everything better is a lie sold to the Church from the very pit of hell. While it is true that Jesus commanded believers in Matthew 22: 37-39, *"You must love the Lord your God with all your heart, all your soul, and all your mind."* This is the first and great commandment. And the second is like it: *"Love your neighbor as yourself."*; however, to love others correctly we must first choose to love God. Love is not just rhetoric, it is action.

The belief somehow that love will stop pain, hatred or violence is contrary to the Bible. Likewise, the belief that a believer must set their biblical convictions aside to accept and include all is a deceptive device perpetrated upon the Church; to not do so somehow makes Christians unloving and elitists. Today's progressive Christianity seeks to condone all behaviors, believe that all mankind are God's children and to portray that there are many ways to salvation and a personal relationship with God. In fact, tenants of this philosophy would have one believe that grace is found in the search for answers and that belief is more valuable in questioning than in absolutes. Additionally, this mindset attempts to look for a group that includes all people, including but not limited to; conventional Christians and doubting skeptics, believers and atheists, men and women, those of all sexual orientations and gender identities and those of all social classes. While we are to love the sinner we are not to accept the sin; neither is the believer to unify oneself with the unbeliever (Amos 3:3). Furthermore, this problematic philosophy attempts to raise the creature above the Creator in their attempt to protect and restore the normality of Earth. Even greater still, this reasoning propagandizes that Jesus is simply one of many ways to experience salvation and completeness of life, and that we can employ diverse sources of knowledge in our spiritual journey. These beliefs and all that carry similar standards are not expressions of love but rather deceptions and distortions of what Jesus spoke and intended through His words. In fact, Jesus told us in Matthew 10:34-37, *"Don't imagine that I came to bring peace to the earth! I came not to bring peace, but a sword. 'I have come to set a man against his father, a daughter against her mother, and a daughter-in-law against her mother-in-law. Your enemies will be right in your own household!' "If you love your father or mother more than you love me, you are not worthy of being mine; or if you love your son or daughter more than me, you are not worthy of being mine."* This does not mean that Jesus was looking for or wanted to bring family dysfunction but what it does mean is that when one truly stands for Christ, they truly stand for what is right and when they understand that one must follow Christ before getting along with others, it will inevitably bring disharmony.

To love someone means to share the truth with them. Regardless of whether it be politically correct, politically expedient or politically acceptable to the masses, love requires truth. While times change and processes change, truth remains constant. If Jesus spoke against certain behaviors in His day, we can be sure He is still opposed to that behavior today. It has been said, *"You will never influence the world by trying to be like it."* Jesus has not called us to be conformed to the world. In fact, he has called us out of the world. To be a light. To be the salt. To make a difference for Him through the way we live. We are to love others but we are to love others by living differently, by sharing the good news of the gospel and the life changing power Jesus brings and by rejecting every new wind of doctrine that blows.

Evette Carter once wrote, *"Conformity is doing what everybody else is doing, regardless of what is right. Morality is doing what is right, regardless of what everybody else is doing."* It's time the Church stopped thinking it could alter one's eternal destiny by accepting another's sin; eternal destiny is altered by the truth of God's word and the messenger that brings it. As Romans 10:14-15 tell us, *"But how can they call on him to save them unless they believe in him? And how can they believe in him if they have never heard about him? And how can they hear about him unless someone tells them? 15 And how will anyone go and tell them without being sent? That is why the Scriptures say, "How beautiful are the feet of messengers who bring good news!""*

Improbable that a sinner has ever been spared the flames of hell by an unimpassioned saint simply trying to sell fire insurance.

Food for Thought

In which ways do I see a comparison between the church of Laodicea and today's American church?

_____

_____

_____

_____

_____

_____

_____

_____

As Evette Carter compared conformity and morality to the masses, what am I doing to avoid conforming to the ills of this world?

_____

_____

_____

_____

_____

_____

_____

Am I more interested in hearing from God through my Pastor or would I rather hear a 'motivational/inspirational' speech (tickling of the ears)? What about hearing from God will strengthen my faith and change my life?

_____

_____

_____

_____

_____

Would God characterize my faith life as complacent and apathetic or vivacious and vigorous? Why? If the former, how can I change this aspect of my faith? Be specific.

_____

_____

_____

_____

_____

_____

_____

_____

_____

Salt is a preservative; it's mission – keep something from going stale. Is my faith and life preserving my culture today? Why or why not?

_____

_____

_____

_____

_____

_____

_____

How can I truly show love and share the Gospel with someone today?

_____

_____

_____

_____

_____

_____

_____

$$\dagger$$

Week 21
THE MAN IN THE MIRROR

That is why we never give up. Though our bodies are dying, our spirits are being renewed every day.
- II Corinthians 4:16

In the 1937 Walt Disney film, Snow White and the Seven Dwarfs, one of the most famous lines takes place as the evil queen stares into the mirror and beckons, *"Hey mirror. Who's the best looking woman in this land?"* While the evil queen simply sought the approval of her physical appearance, this is a question that so many seek the answer to daily. Whether it be the individual that looks into the mirror, no longer seeing the young person that once stood before him, but now seeing one in whom the years have taken their toll or the young boy that sees himself in the image of his father, the mirror simply reflects back what the outer man is or has become. While there is not much that can be done to halt genetics or time, the reflection one should be more focused on is the inner man. Just like the mirror reflects the image of the outward man so the Bible serves as a daily reflection of the inner man and our constant pursuit to become more like its author – Christ.

The Bible describes for us an excellent example of the value that man places on the exterior as opposed to the value that God imparts on the interior. In I Samuel 16 we read how God sent Samuel to anoint the man who would become the successor to King Saul. As Samuel made his way to Bethlehem he was instructed to find Jesse, and there it would be revealed to him as to which son would be anointed the future king of Israel. Upon Samuel's arrival he called the men of the city to sacrifice to the Lord. As Jesse's son Eliab approached, Samuel thought to himself, *"This must be the one"*. Eliab was the oldest son of Jesse and he was a big and rugged man but he would not be the one that God had chosen. As each of the brothers subsequently passed before Samuel, each was turned away. As Samuel began to wonder who God had selected and what this man would possess over the obvious outward attributes of the previous, God spoke to Samuel and reminded him that He did not care about what the outward appearance wrought; it was the inner part that mattered to Him.

After each of Jesse's sons had come before Samuel and had been turned away, Samuel asked Jesse, *"Are these all the sons you have?"* Jesse replied, *"There's still the youngest, but he's out in the fields watching the sheep and goats."* - I Samuel 16:11. Assuredly Samuel must have thought, *"Well it can't be him. There's no way God would make a mere boy king of Israel. There must be some kind of mix up."* But nevertheless, Samuel told Jesse to go get him.

As David approached from the fields Samuel noticed how

good-looking a young man he was but more so how the Spirit of God was upon him. At the moment God told Samuel, *"This is the one; anoint him."* - I Samuel 16:12. As Samuel anointed the future king of Israel he recalled the words that God had spoken to him just moments before when He said, *"Don't judge by his appearance or height, for I have rejected him. The Lord doesn't see things the way you see them. People judge by outward appearance, but the Lord looks at the heart."* - I Samuel 16:7.

History shows how David would go on to become Israel's foremost king, barring none but the Lord Jesus Himself who would come through the very lineage of David. Even more, David is the only man in history where God records that *"I have found David son of Jesse, a man after my own heart. He will do everything I want him to do."* - Acts 13:22. When Samuel first followed God's command and went looking for the next king of Israel, he would never have chosen David in a line-up but fortunately God is never concerned with the outward appearance. Whether one is young or old, man or woman, rich or poor, educated or not, short or tall, black, white, yellow, brown or red, God doesn't care. What He does care about is the state of our heart and our relationship with Him. For this He has given us His word which should serve as the metrics for lives.

If we desire to look into the mirror and ask, *"Mirror, mirror, on the wall, who's the fairest of them all?"* Lord willing the answer in turn will be, *"The Lord Jesus and you in Him."* Let us not wait till we grow old that we look in the mirror and wonder who is staring back. Start now. Start today seeking to reflect the Lord

Jesus; age should not be a limitation.

"Don't let anyone think less of you because you are young. Be an example to all believers in what you say, in the way you live, in your love, your faith, and your purity" - I Timothy 4:12.

Food for Thought

Am I happy with the faith reflection I see in the spiritual mirror? What does the reflection look like?

_____

_____

_____

_____

_____

_____

How would my spiritual mirror respond upon seeing my faith reflection?

_____

_____

_____

_____

_____

_____

Am I more focused on the exterior of others or do I remember each is an eternal soul Christ died for? If so, what am I doing about it?

_____

_____

_____

_____

_____

_____

_____

The attribute that allowed David to face down a giant and later become king was that of faith – faith in God. Am I hampering this faith growth because I am concerned with what others say or am I clinging to God's words, *"Don't judge by his appearance or height"*, realizing God can overcome any perceived deficiency?

_____

_____

_____

_____

_____

_____

_____

Think about David's lineage. Great kings throughout history leading to the apex of Jesus Christ. It can be argued that faith was the reason David was chosen and his seed was blessed. What will future generations say about the faith I exhibited? Will my family remain strong and centered on Christ or will my lack of faith lead to heartache and ruin? The Bible says, *"After that generation died, another generation grew up who did not acknowledge the LORD or remember the mighty things he had done for Israel."* - Judges 2:10. Faith and the transfer of faith makes all the difference. What am I doing today to transfer my faith to others?

_____

_____

_____

_____

_____

_____

_____

_____

_____

_____

Week 22
PRAYER CLOSET CONDITIONING

But when you pray, go away by yourself, shut the door behind you, and pray to your Father in private. Then your Father, who sees everything, will reward you.
- Matthew 6:6

Martin Luther once described the reaction of his pup as it wandered over to his table. He goes on to say that the pup looked up, he looked down and he looked all around for just a nibble from his master's hands. Then he eagerly awaited, awaited a morsel to fall from the table, while remaining completely mesmerized on his master. Luther continued to describe the dog's behavior saying, *"Oh, if I could only pray the way this dog watches the meat! All his thoughts are concentrated on the piece of meat. Otherwise he has no thought, wish or hope".*

Prayer ought to be the way that Luther describes his dog's behavior; mesmerized, salivating, emptied of oneself and completely focused on the object of our attention and adoration, God Himself. Dr. Ralph Martin best described the topic of prayer in the Bible as *"at root, simply paying attention to God"*. Prayer should not only focus on our requests and needs, but prayer is how we reenergize our souls in a spirit of thankfulness through a complete dependency on our Heavenly Father. Prayer is the medicine that fuels the believer much like spinach fueled Popeye, while at the same time a lack of prayer to the believer is like Superman being confronted with kryptonite. E.M. Bounds painted the picture this way, *"What the Church needs today is not more machinery or better, not new organizations or more novel methods, but men whom the Holy Ghost can use--men of prayer, men mighty in prayer."*

Prayer is the medicine that fuels the believer much like spinach fueled Popeye...

Our enemy, Satan, is described as a *"lion seeking to destroy"*, so how is it then with such an adversary that as believers we ignore and reject the power found through prayer? When one disregards their personal, private time in the prayer closet before beginning one's day it is as a soldier heading to the battlefield while leaving his weapon, helmet and flak jacket at base camp. It is irrational and beyond belief that one could think he will win or even survive when going into battle defenseless. Famous

Civil War General, Robert E. Lee, once remarked, *"Knowing that intercessory prayer is our mightiest weapon and the supreme call for all Christians today, I pleadingly urge our people everywhere to pray. Believing that prayer is the greatest contribution that our people can make in this critical hour, I humbly urge that we take time to pray--to really pray. Let there be prayer at sunup, at noonday, at sundown, at midnight--all through the day. Let us all pray for our children, our youth, our aged, our pastors, our homes. Let us pray for our churches. Let us pray for ourselves, that we may not lose the word 'concern' out of our Christian vocabulary. Let us pray for our nation. Let us pray for those who have never known Jesus Christ and redeeming love, for moral forces everywhere, for our national leaders. Let prayer be our passion. Let prayer be our practice."*

The battle we are engaged in and the enemy we face are not new to Christ's bride but the lack of passion to pray and the disbelief in the power of it all seem to be at an all-time high. All one needs to do is to look around with eyes wide open and he will see the dismal, deteriorating circumstances within our world. Today is no different than in the apostles' day when they were faced with the onslaught of persecution in the fact that the way they found strength to stand was kneeling in prayer before the One who could save them. Through the centuries there have been stalwarts of the faith who have known, experienced and exemplified the power of prayer. In fact, Martin Luther once said, *"If I should neglect prayer but a single day, I should lose a great deal of the fire of faith."* As a car engine needs fuel to run, as the human body needs food to thrive so the soul needs time alone in prayer with God to replenish. Prayer is not only what the church needs, it is not only what the world needs, prayer is what each individual needs. If we are to see the Lord perform mighty acts in and through our lives it will all begin in the prayer closet of our lives. If we are unwilling to put in the time in secret, we will never experience the magnificent feats in public.

Remember, as Thomas Watson once remarked, *"The angel fetched Peter out of prison, but it was prayer that fetched the angel."*

Food for Thought

How intense and focused is my prayer life? Do I pray believing or hoping? The Bible says, *"And it is impossible to please God without faith."* - Hebrew 11:6.

_____

_____

_____

_____

_____

_____

_____

_____

_____

Is my prayer life in need of life support or is it vibrant and healthy? Why or Why Not? How can I resuscitate it?

_____

_____

_____

_____

_____

_____

_____

_____

Do I pray for others or does my prayer life look like a wish list to God for myself?

_____

_____

_____

_____

_____

_____

Is my prayer/faith life between me and God or do I attempt to garner the approval and praise of man? *"When you pray, don't be like the hypocrites who love to pray publicly on street corners and in the synagogues where everyone can see them. I tell you the truth that is all the reward they will ever get. But when you pray, go away by yourself, shut the door behind you, and pray to your Father in private. Then your Father, who sees everything, will reward you."*

"When you pray, don't babble on and on as the Gentiles do. They think their prayers are answered merely by repeating their words again and again. Don't be like them, for your Father knows exactly what you need even before you ask him!" - Matthew 6:5-8.

_____

_____

_____

_____

_____

_____

_____

_____

_____

_____

Begin keeping a prayer journal. (Petition, date requested, date answered, how did God answer my prayer.) A history of seeing how and when God answers prayer will strengthen my resolve to prayer and my faith in God.

✝

Week 23
IDENTITY LOSS

*It was at Antioch that the believers
were first called Christians.*
- Acts 11:26b

A long standing symbol of the union that occurs between a man and a woman during marriage is that of name changing; the legal action where a bride takes her husband's last name. This idea stems all the way back to Genesis 2:24 where we read, *"This explains why a man leaves his father and mother and is joined to his wife, and the two are united into one."* However today, many women are choosing to forsake this action of unity. In fact, in 2014, it was reported that 29.5 percent of new brides decided to keep their maiden name, an increase from 26 percent in 2000. What does this say about the commitment being made? Are women choosing to keep their name and forsake taking that of their husband due to the uncertainty of success in marriage? Or does it proclaim a deeper message of individualism? Either way, as believers when we decide to unite with Christ we are no longer to herald our name. Quite the opposite, we are to lose our identity in Him.

II Corinthians 5:17, a very familiar verse reminds us of our true identity as we read, *"This means that anyone who belongs to Christ has become a new person. The old life is gone; a new life has begun!"* As believers our lives are no longer our own; we have been purchased and thus now belong to Christ. A long-time tradition among slaves recorded how they would take the name of their master – in essence, losing their identity in another. Just as in the book of Philemon, Paul wrote on behalf of Onesimus, a servant who was a run away, *"Onesimus hasn't been of much use to you in the past, but now he is very useful to both of us"* and further says, *"It seems you lost Onesimus for a little while so that you could have him back forever. He is no longer like a slave to you. He is more than a slave, for he is a beloved brother, especially to me. Now he will mean much more to you, both as a man and as a brother in the Lord."* - Philemon 1:11-16.

Names can bring prestige, power, authority, respect and so many other attributes; but a name also brings responsibility and a sense of loyalty and pride. Similar to the many brides today who are choosing to keep their name, regardless the reason, Christians are trapped in a mindset of believing they have the right to live their lives as they see fit. However, as a believer we are a representative of Jesus Christ. There is an old expression that says, *"You are the only Bible that some may read"*. If this is accurate, what does our life say about the God of the Bible? Do people see Him or does He become muffled under the roar of our pride?

There's a story told about a renowned artist, Paul Gustave Dore (1821-1883), who lost his passport while traveling in Europe. When he came to a border crossing, he explained his situation to one of the guards. As he told them who he was, he hoped that would be enough and that he would allowed to pass. The guard, however, accused him saying that many people attempted to cross the border by claiming to be someone they were not. Dore insisted that he was the man he claimed to be. *"All right,"* said the official, *"we'll give you a test, and if you pass it we'll let you through."* Handing him a pencil and a sheet of paper, he told the artist to sketch several folks standing nearby. Dore did it so quickly and skillfully that the guard was convinced he was indeed who he claimed to be. His work confirmed his word!

In today's world many people will refuse to listen to what we have to say until they watch our lives – if our actions don't support our words that will be the end. There are many commercials that advertise protection against identity theft, and we should be very careful as to how that impacts us. But we also need to remember that identity loss in the One who gave Himself for us is not only a privilege but an obligation. Our lives are no longer about us (as if they ever were); they are about reflecting the face of our heavenly Father.

Most people will not purposefully disgrace their human families or tarnish the family name, so why is that we don't live our spiritual lives in the same manner? Today's Church has become so influenced by the world that we accept Christ's forgiveness and promise of a home in heaven but still believe that our lives belong to us and are for our enjoyment, in whatever way we choose. However, if like the artist, we were approached and asked to show our 'credentials' for calling ourselves Christians, would the practical mirror the contextual? Expressed another way, if we were to be put on trial for being a Christian, would there be enough evidence to convict?

Who do we belong to today, God or ourselves? If we choose God, then why are we so focused on other's knowing who we are? Let us strive as Paul wrote, *"that I may know Him and the power of His resurrection..."* For when we know Who's we are, it no longer matters who we are.

Food for Thought

How do I strive to hide my life in the shadow of the cross or do I live to shine a spotlight of attention upon myself?

_____

_____

_____

_____

_____

As humans we all have a desire to know we are unique and that our life is significant. However, as a believer my life should be about loving God and loving others. What can I do for someone this week to model Christ and to forsake my own ambitions?

_____

_____

_____

_____

_____

_____

From a very real practical standpoint, if I am married, do I put my spouse's needs in front of mine or is life lived for me? How is the health of my marriage/relationship? What can I do this week to show my spouse my life's goal is to love and please him/her?

_____

_____

_____

_____

_____

_____

_____

The Bible tells us in Revelation 2:17, *"Anyone with ears to hear must listen to the Spirit and understand what he is saying to the churches. To everyone who is victorious I will give some of the manna that has been hidden away in heaven. And I will give to each one a white stone, and on the stone will be engraved a new name that no one understands except the one who receives it."* If God was to give me a new name today, describing my life, what would I hope He would say? What do I need to start doing today so that my life would align with Christ's words?

_____

_____

_____

_____

_____

_____

The number one name that can be given us is Christian (Christ follower). Do my actions and lifestyle align with the characteristics and attributes of Christ? Why or why not? How can I change to ensure I am not a hypocrite?

_____

_____

_____

_____

_____

_____

A THOUSAND HILLS
WORTH OF CATTLE

For all the animals of the forest are mine,
and I own the cattle on a thousand hills.
- Psalm 50:10

Money is a funny thing, the more one has the more one seems to chase. One of the largest lottery jackpots was recorded at $1.5 billion. The statistical analysis had the odds of winning at 1 in 292.2 million. It was also determined that one would have a better chance of flipping a coin and having it land on heads 28 consecutive times as opposed to winning the lottery. Furthermore, if one was to buy a lottery ticket each week, the probability of winning would be once every 269,000 years. Even in the face of such daunting and dismal odds, this didn't keep people from playing and dreaming about how so much money could be spent. For most people who live paycheck to paycheck, never quite sure how the bills will be paid, let alone the possibility of saving for retirement, the thought of becoming independently wealthy is only a dream. While we dream of money beyond compare, the truth is we have the privilege of getting to know the One who owns it all.

The concept of money is discussed in great detail with probably no more intensity than the passage that is most often taken out of context, *"For the love of money is the root of all kinds of evil. And some people, craving money, have wandered from the true faith and pierced themselves with many sorrows"* - I Timothy 6:10. Another text says, *"No one can serve two masters. For you will hate one and love the other; you will be devoted to one and despise the other. You cannot serve both God and money"* - Matthew 6:24. However, the passage that I believe most directly speaks to how we ought to view money and possessions is found in Matthew 6:19-21, *"Don't store up treasures here on earth, where moths eat them and rust destroys them, and where thieves break in and steal. Store your treasures in heaven, where moths and rust cannot destroy, and thieves do not break in and steal. Wherever your treasure is, there the desires of your heart will also be."* There is nothing inherently wrong with money as it is a means to live life but when the pursuit of the almighty dollar becomes the single most important facet of life, we have set it up as a god and the end is in the waiting. Early Church Father, John Chrysostom, once commented about the pursuit of money as, *"A dreadful thing is the love of money! It disables both eyes and ears, and makes men worse to deal with than a wild beast, allowing a man to consider neither conscience nor friendship nor fellowship nor salvation."*

Many folks find the desire for extra money to be an appealing nudge. Money allows one to cover basic life needs, to have comfort and experience leisure and to believe they are secure whatever will come, but no amount of money will do a thing for a person beyond this physical world. The story is told in Luke 16:19-31 about the rich man and Lazarus. In this life the rich man had everything he needed and everything he ever wanted while Lazarus had to beg for the scraps that fell from the rich man's table. However, in the life to come the rich man found himself in hell while Lazarus went to be with the Lord in Abraham's bosom. The blessing or curse of having or not having money was not the underlying reason for where either one found themselves but the love for, attention paid to and the pursuit after money is what caused the rich man to ignore his need for salvation; he simply thought he could purchase it like everything else. To this point Jesus said, *"In fact, it is easier for a camel to go through the eye of a needle than for a rich person to enter the Kingdom of God!"* - Luke 18:25.

Our God doesn't need our finances and He doesn't want our finances; what He wants is a relationship with each of us.

The act of dreaming what it would be like to win the lottery is fascinating and entertaining. Just as the act of worrying about not having enough money or the act of elevating the chase to earn more money above God will not change one thing for the better in our lives. In fact, we read in Matthew 10:29-31, *"What is the price of two sparrows—one copper coin? But not a single sparrow can fall to the ground without your Father knowing it. And the very hairs on your head are all numbered. So don't be afraid; you are more valuable to God than a whole flock of sparrows."*

Paul Chappell once remarked about the role and relationship of God, money and man as, *"God does not need your money; He wants what it represents-you. Finances are God's gift to you to fulfill His will for your life. While God desires you to prioritize His work in giving, He wants you to purpose to follow and serve Him no matter what happens with your finances."*

Our God doesn't need our finances and He doesn't want our finances; what He wants is a relationship with each of us. Once we accept Him and our relationship begins we should never again be concerned with our daily provision. Let us remember our God owns everything and He is waiting to provide all we will ever need. All we need to do is to ask – *"Don't worry about anything; instead, pray about everything. Tell God what you need, and thank him for all he has done"* -Philippians 4:6.

Food for Thought

What is the focus of my attention? The pursuit for materialism or the pursuit to become like Christ? How do my actions support my belief?

_____

_____

_____

_____

_____

_____

_____

_____

The Bible teaches in Matthew 6:24, *"No one can serve two masters. For you will hate one and love the other; you will be devoted to one and despise the other. You cannot serve God and be enslaved to money."* Who is my master – God or things? If I asked my family and friends, what would they say? Most of all, what would God say?

_____

_____

_____

_____

_____

_____

Name the ways in which I worry about my daily needs. Name what needs to change so I trust God to provide.

_____

_____

_____

_____

_____

_____

_____

Am I good steward of God's possessions? How do I use what God has given me to further His kingdom? Not just with my finances but with the skills, talents and abilities and so on He has given me.

_____

_____

_____

_____

_____

_____

_____

How can I expect God to 'give me more' when I don't use appropriately what I already have?

_____

_____

_____

_____

_____

_____

The Bible tells us in Luke 12:48, _"When someone has been given much, much will be required in return; and when someone has been entrusted with much, even more will be required."_ What is God requiring from my life? Am I willing to 'pay the price'?

_____

_____

_____

_____

_____

_____

_____

_____

_____

_____

✝

Week 25
REFINED THROUGH THE FIRE

"Look!" Nebuchadnezzar shouted. "I see four men, unbound, walking around in the fire unharmed! And the fourth looks like a god!"
- Daniel 3:25

American author Archibald Rutledge (1883-1973) tells the story of a man who was employed in one of the great forests of the South and the relationship between him and his dog. The man's faithful dog had been burned to death as an intense fire raced through and destroyed the forest. Rutledge noted how the little dog had been caught under a tree in an attempt to guard his master's dinner pail; and though the flames raged fierce, the little guy wouldn't leave it even as the flames reverberated around him. The man was heart-broken when he found the scorched remains of his little companion. With an inability to control his emotions and tears inexplicably heard in his voice, he said: *"I always had to be careful what I told him to do, because I knew he would do it."* This is exactly the level of obedience to which we have been commanded to follow. As believers we are to model the example of obedience Jesus demonstrated when He would not even allow the cross to interfere with what the Father had commanded.

We read in Daniel 3 about three young men who were willing to defy the authority of their day because of their unrelenting commitment to God. This is a famous passage, probably one of the most well-known Bible stories; Shadrach, Meshach and Abednego in the fiery furnace. Much like the loyal dog in the opening illustration, these three young men exhibited extreme levels of faithfulness, conviction and fearlessness in the face of certain and immediate death. These men were not willing to compromise or ignore what they knew and believed to be right despite the irreversible consequences that would come their way. Such conviction is seldom found in adults let alone in teenagers!

As we read their proclamation of peace and trust with whatever the outcome may be, their response was, *"O Nebuchadnezzar, we do not need to defend ourselves before you. If we are thrown into the blazing furnace, the God whom we serve is able to save us. He will rescue us from your power, Your Majesty. But even if he doesn't, we want to make it clear to you, Your Majesty, that we will never serve your gods or worship the gold statue you have set up"* (vss. 16-18). True faith in God is knowing He is capable of directing an outcome while accepting whatever outcome He allows.

I recall hearing a story about a man who had a specific outcome in mind but who was also willing to accept whatever the outcome would reveal. As a boat was crossing Lake Michigan carrying him toward Milwaukee a terrible storm arose. The guests on the boat were terrified, screaming and pacing back and forth, while the man remained calm and secure. As one guest began to take notice of the man's calm demeanor, she was overcome with a desire to know how he could keep his cool. After asking him about the situation, his response was, *"I've got one son in Illinois and the other is in Heaven. As my plan is to see the one in Illinois, and possibly take in a ball game, my desire is to see either. It really isn't up to me; you see, it doesn't matter which one I see."*

This is the kind of tenacious faith that these three young Jewish men exhibited in the face of a godless, callous society. Despite the persecution and ultimate execution, they would have to face, their resolve remained impervious to the pressure and consequences of their actions. Charles Spurgeon once noted, *"Fiery trials make golden Christians"*. This summation approves the ideal, belief and ultimate truth that when one is in the will of God and chooses to follow regardless of the repercussions, God does not leave us alone but, in fact, walks side by side with us through the trial as exhibited in verse 25, *"Look!"* Nebuchadnezzar shouted. *"I see four men, unbound, walking around in the fire unharmed! And the fourth looks like a god!"*

Fiery trials are as present today as they were in the days of Shadrach, Meshach and Abednego but so is the victorious presence of God. In fact, we read in I Peter 4:12-13, *"Dear friends, don't be surprised at the fiery trials you are going through, as if something strange were happening to you. Instead, be very glad— for these trials make you partners with Christ in his suffering, so that you will have the wonderful joy of seeing his glory when it is revealed to all the world."*

Therefore, as fire refines precious elements, let us realize the fiery trials we endure are there to refine our lives and to make us more like Christ. Always remember as James Faust once wrote, *"Here then is a great truth. In the pain, the agony, and the heroic endeavors of life, we pass through a refiner's fire, so the insignificant and the unimportant in our lives can melt away like dross and make our faith bright, intact, and strong".*

Food for Thought

What fire am I walking through today? Am I using the trials to allow God to refine and strengthen my faith or am I using it to define me as a victim?

_____

_____

_____

_____

_____

_____

_____

What type of counsel am I eliciting? Those like Job's friends who provided strong counsel, *"But now when trouble strikes, you lose heart. You are terrified when it touches you. Doesn't your reverence for God give you confidence? Doesn't your life of integrity give you hope?" "Stop and think!"* - Job 4:5-7 or like Job's wife who said, *"Are you still trying to maintain your integrity? Curse God and die."* - Job 2:9. What needs to change?

_____

_____

_____

_____

_____

_____

_____

How will this circumstance/ordeal strengthen my faith and better equip me to help others?

_____

_____

_____

_____

_____

_____

_____

What do I suppose would 'tip my scale' and cause me to lose faith?

_____

_____

_____

_____

_____

If presented with a situation like Shadrach, Meshach and Abednego, would I be willing to stand for my faith regardless the outcome?

_____

_____

_____

_____

_____

✝

Week 26

THE TRUMPET'S BLAST

It will happen in a moment, in the blink of an eye, when the last trumpet is blown. For when the trumpet sounds, those who have died will be raised to live forever. And we who are living will also be transformed.
- I Corinthians 15:52

I once heard from a story from a preacher about a father and his little boy which took place immediately following the end of the boy's Sunday school class. The teacher had been focusing on Jesus' return. While the little boy couldn't grasp everything about what the teacher taught, the boy's response does demonstrate the need to be ready regardless of the day or time.

He said, *"Daddy, do you believe Jesus is coming back?"*
With that the father responded, *"Of course buddy."*
To that the little investigator asked, *"Will it be soon?"*
As the father thought he replied, *"Maybe."*
Still not quite appeased, the little guy persisted, *"How about*

today?"

The father continued to absorb his son's line of questioning and with a gleam in his eyes, he said, *"Hopefully."*

As the little guy took note of his father's joy, he simply said, *"Daddy, I want to be ready."*

While we are not sure of the day or the hour, the one thing we can be sure of, just as sure as we are here today, is that Jesus is coming back and the countdown to His return is closing.

When asked about the time of His return Jesus described it in Matthew 24:37-44 as, *"When the Son of Man returns, it will be like it was in Noah's day. In those days before the flood, the people were enjoying banquets and parties and weddings right up to the time Noah entered his boat. People didn't realize what was going to happen until the flood came and swept them all away. That is the way it will be when the Son of Man comes. Two men will be working together in the field; one will be taken, the other left. Two women will be grinding flour at the mill; one will be taken, the other left. So you, too, must keep watch! For you don't know what day your Lord is coming. Understand this: If a homeowner knew exactly when a burglar was coming, he would keep watch and not permit his house to be broken into. You also must be ready all the time, for the Son of Man **will come when least expected."***

In the military there are two distinct functions of the cornet (trumpet). The first is the playing of *"Taps"* which occurs at the end of the day and also in remembrance of those who have paid the ultimate price of laying down their lives in protection of our country. The other occurrence is the playing of *"Revelry"*. This is played each morning as the troops rise for the start of another day and has for a long time been the sound announcing a forward military move or 'Charge'. When we think about these two uses and melodies performed, we can think back to the day that Jesus laid down His life on the cross as the ultimate payment for all of mankind's sin. One can imagine an angel of the heavenly armies standing on a nearby hill playing *"Taps"* as our Lord and Savior took His final breath. On the other hand, regarding the battle cry of *"Revelry"*, only a mere three days earlier the same angel who stood playing *"Taps"* on that lonesome hill now stood erect on top of the grave declaring the victorious 'charge' or rising of this same Lord and Savior; who had now defeated the enemies that had looked to extinguish His life and lifesaving power. This same revelry that declared the resurgence of life and victory so many years ago will be the same revelry that will announce the coming again of the Commander of the heavenly hosts to unite Himself with His people.

While we are not sure of the day or the hour, the one thing we can be sure of, just as sure as we are here today, is that Jesus is coming back and the countdown to His return is closing.

Just as an army does not announce its impending advance until the moment of attack, so will be the announcing of the King of kings and Prince of Peace. While Jesus Himself let us know that no man *"knows the day or the hour"*, He has given signs that will foreshadow His return so that no one has reason to be ill-prepared. Just as it was prophesied thousands of years ago that Jesus would come to give His life and each prophesy was fulfilled to the minute detail, so will be the appearing of Jesus again to receive His own *"so that you will always be with me where I am"* - John 14:3.

The first time Jesus came it was as a babe in a manger, the next time He comes it will as the Bridegroom receiving His bride. The first time Jesus came it was as a servant to all, the next time He comes it will be as the King of kings. The first time Jesus came it was as the Passover lamb, the next time He comes it will be as the Lion of Judah. The first time Jesus came it was as a man of sorrows, the next time He comes it will be as the bright Morning Star. The first time Jesus came it was as the firstborn among many brothers, the firstborn from the dead and the root and offspring of David, the next time He comes it will be as the Righteous Judge, the Chief Shepherd and the Prince of Peace. *"He who is the faithful witness to all these things says, "Yes, I am coming soon!" Amen! Come, Lord Jesus!"* - Rev. 22:20.

Food for Thought

Am I ready for Christ's return? What if it were today? Describe what I would do different if I really believed Jesus might return today?

_____

_____

_____

_____

_____

_____

_____

Am I actively *"being about His business"* or have I sat back with my feet up? Are my family and friends ready for Christ's return? What am I doing to ensure they are?

_____

_____

_____

_____

_____

_____

_____

_____

What am I doing with the time God gives me to live for Him? Be specific.

_____

_____

_____

_____

_____

_____

_____

_____

List the signs of His coming according to scripture. Without knowing the exact day Christ will return, does any other prophetic promise need to happen?

_____

_____

_____

_____

_____

_____

_____

_____

_____

The Bible tells us in II Timothy 4:8, *"And now the prize awaits me--the crown of righteousness, which the Lord, the righteous Judge, will give me on the day of his return. And the prize is not just for me but for all who eagerly look forward to his appearing."* Am I looking forward to and anticipating hearing the Lord's trumpet or have I become comfy in this world?

_____

_____

_____

_____

_____

_____

_____

Week 27
WAITING FOR THE CAVALRY TO ARRIVE

I heard the size of their army, which was 200 million mounted troops.
- Revelation 9:16

The Battle of the Alamo is a U.S. history lesson and story that demonstrates the resolve of the American spirit and also the importance of having a supporting force in battle. Unfortunately for those brave Texans that would not surrender the Alamo, a pivotal point in the battle for Texas, the cavalry would not arrive in time to save the fort or the lives of those courageous patriots within. As history records, on February 23, 1836, a Mexican force comprising somewhere between 1,800 and 6,000 men, commanded by General Antonio Lopez de Santa Anna, began a siege of the fort. The Texans, inclusive of names like Colonel James Bowie, Lt. Colonel William Travis, Davy Crockett and an estimated 179-254 others held out for 13 days, but on the morning of March 6 Mexican forces broke through a breach in the outer wall of the courtyard and overpowered them. Santa Anna ordered his men to take no prisoners, yet a small handful of the Texans were spared and sent to General Sam Houston's camp in Gonzalez with a warning that a similar fate awaited the rest of the Texans if they continued their revolt. This would prove to be a disastrous move on the part of Santa Anna. For on April 21, 1836, Sam Houston and some 800 Texans defeated Santa Anna's Mexican force of 1,500 men at San Jacinto shouting *"Remember the Alamo!"* as they attacked. The victory ensured the success of Texan independence. Furthermore, Santa Anna, who had been taken prisoner, came to terms with Houston to end the war. In May, Mexican troops in San Antonio were ordered to withdraw, and to demolish the Alamo's fortifications as they went.

A mighty army can be the difference between winning and losing, victory or defeat. And even in cases where one army may be outnumbered by another, numbers aren't the only determining factor in battle. There are many stories throughout history that demonstrate the importance of conceptual military strategies and the desire to protect one's homeland. However, in the end, the size of an army can certainly attribute to the victory that is secured.

The Christian life can many times feel like the battle of the Alamo; we are outnumbered, our weapons and defenses seem inferior to that of the enemy; and we are wondering when the reinforcements will arrive. The battle is surreal and our will to keep fighting seems to drain with every attack. We know what God's word teaches about putting on the armor of God, how the battle is the Lord's and that He has already won the war;

we also know that the enemy is treacherous and powerful but the causalities continue to occur daily at astounding levels. When will it be over? When will the Lord return and defeat the enemy once and for all? These are common and legitimate questions. Just like the defenders of the Alamo longed for the appearance of Houston's army to deliver them from certain death, we long for the return of Christ to vanquish the enemies of God who seek to attack and destroy all that we are fighting for.

In II Chronicles 20, we read of another story of unbelievable odds and an enormous army that would seemingly decimate the nation of Israel. Verse 2 tells us how, *"Messengers came and told Jehoshaphat, 'A vast army from Edom is marching against you from beyond the Dead Sea.'"* As with many people, this would be an unimaginable threat that would cause one to worry, distress and ponder the appropriate course of action but the Bible tells us that Jehoshaphat took the matter in prayer to the Captain of Hosts who was the One and only that could bring about safety and victory for the Israelites. At the conclusion of his prayer we catch a glimpse of how God would raise up a valiant warrior who would take the fight to the enemy and prevail in victory.

For certain, the name Jahrzeit is unknown to most; but the Bible tells us how the Spirit of the Lord came upon him leading him to exclaim the *"Remember the Alamo!"* type cry to the people thus inspiring and leading them to victory. In verses 15-17 Jahaziel told the people, *"He said, 'Listen, all you people of Judah and Jerusalem! Listen, King Jehoshaphat! This is what the Lord says: Do not be afraid! Don't be discouraged by this mighty* army, *for the battle is not yours, but God's. Tomorrow, march out against them. You will find them coming up through the ascent of Ziz at the end of the valley that opens into the wilderness of Jeruel. But you will not even need to fight. Take your positions; then stand still and watch the Lord's victory. He is with you, O people of Judah and Jerusalem. Do not be afraid or discouraged. Go out against them tomorrow, for the Lord is with you!"* This man understood that the battle was not his to win or even fight, the Lord of Hosts was providing the force, the cavalry and the power to extinguish the enemy.

Whether one is a professional soldier or a member of a rag-tag band of volunteers, the hope we have as believers is that we do not fight alone. As we read in Exodus 14:14, *"The LORD himself will fight for you. Just stay calm."* The Lord Jesus is coming back – soon! Until then let us stand strong knowing the cavalry is in route.

Food for Thought

How's my daily faith fight going? Am I holding ground, taking ground, or losing ground? Why? Be specific.

_____

_____

_____

_____

_____

Am I utilizing the weapons of the faith I've have been given? (Eph. 6) Why and How? Why not? How can I change this to go on the offense?

_____

_____

_____

_____

_____

_____

_____

At this point in my faith fight, would I be more likely to be compared to the men at the Alamo experiencing the enemy's attack of General Sam Houston mounting an attack against the enemy? Why?

_____

_____

_____

_____

_____

_____

_____

Do I consult the military strategy manual (the Bible) daily or am I attempting to fight the enemy in my own strength and ability?

_____

_____

_____

_____

_____

Am I fearing, distressing and agonizing over the enemy and his attacks or am I claiming the promise of God found in Colossians 1:13, "_For he has rescued us from the kingdom of darkness and transferred us into the Kingdom of his dear Son,?_" What strategies should I adopt to strengthen my faith fight?

_____

_____

_____

_____

_____

_____

_____

_____

Week 28
GET OFF GOD'S THRONE

...and the Ancient One sat down to judge.
His clothing was as white as snow, his hair like
purest wool. He sat on a fiery throne
with wheels of blazing fire.
- Daniel 7:9

Every one of us has dealt with this issue or are dealing with this issue - elevating ourselves while removing God from His rightful position of King. Before one accepts Jesus as Savior, man acts as king of his own life, but once one has humbled himself to accept Christ's sacrifice as the perfect and only atonement for his sins. It is then our daily duty to remove ourselves from the throne of our hearts and in its place uplift Christ.

We read a story in Daniel 4 about the Babylonian king Nebuchadnezzar and the price he paid for rejecting the warning of unabated pride. Nebuchadnezzar's empire had grown to be the grandest, wealthiest and most powerful entity of its time and actually one of the top 7 empires throughout history. Verse 22 records for us, *"That tree, Your Majesty, is you. For you have grown strong and great; your greatness reaches up to heaven, and your rule to the ends of the earth."* However, all of this caused Nebuchadnezzar to believe he was the reason for the empire's success despite warnings presented by Daniel on God's behalf. In fact, Daniel admonishes the king in verse 27 to *"Break from your wicked past and be merciful to the poor. Perhaps then you will continue to prosper."* Unfortunately, pride is a stranglehold that entraps many a man and pulls him down to discipline, death and destruction.

As the story unfolds, we read of the fate that pride caused and the payment that Nebuchadnezzar would be required to pay. In verses 31-33 we see how once again, God's warning and man's refusal to repent, would collide on a one-way route with complete and utter destruction for man. We read, *"While these words were still in his mouth, a voice called down from heaven, 'O King Nebuchadnezzar, this message is for you! You are no longer ruler of this kingdom. You will be driven from human society. You will live in the fields with the wild animals, and you will eat grass like a cow. Seven periods of time will pass while you live this way, until you learn that the Most High rules over the kingdoms of the world and gives them to anyone he chooses.' That same hour the judgment was fulfilled, and Nebuchadnezzar was driven from human society. He ate grass like a cow, and he was drenched with the dew of heaven. He lived this way until his hair was as long as eagles' feathers and his nails were like birds' claws."* That very hour the word was fulfilled concerning Nebuchadnezzar; he was driven from men and ate grass like oxen; his body was wet with the dew of heaven till his hair had grown like eagles' feathers and his nails like birds' claws. For the next 7 years Nebuchadnezzar would live, not just among the animals, but as an animal. His total existence is what paints the picture for our current day werewolf. This king, who was the pinnacle of power and wealth, was now reduced to solitary, insanity and destitution because of a self-inflated image described as, *"Look at this great city of Babylon! By my own mighty power, I have built this beautiful city as my royal residence to display my majestic splendor."*

As exhibited here, pride may be the most destructive temptation and sin that befalls man. Recall, it was the sin of pride that brought down Lucifer from the courts of heaven to a prophesied final destination in the lake of fire. It was the sin of pride that caused Adam and Eve to forsake unimaginable beauty in an effort to be *"as God"*. It was the sin of pride that would cause one brother to take the life of another because of a veiled attempt of obedience to God's command of sacrifice. It was the sin of pride that would cause Abraham to become entwined in an inappropriate relationship to father a child, instead of trusting God to fulfill His covenant. It was the sin of Moses in striking a rock that would seal his fate and prevent him from entering God's Promised Land. And it is the sin of pride that causes a man to reject Christ as Lord and Savior in an attempt to do it on his own.

The Bible has much to say on this issue. Proverbs 16:18 tells us, *"Pride goes before destruction, and haughtiness before a fall"* while Proverbs 29:23 says, *"Pride ends in humiliation, while humility brings honor."* From the example of Nebuchadnezzar in Babylon to our very own hearts, pride will destroy as a cancer. As believers, it is not simply enough that Christ is our Savior; He needs to be our King. That means every day we need to step down from the throne and put Christ on it until He is ultimately and absolutely and forever King of our lives.

Food for Thought

Who's on the throne of my life? How long has it been?

_____

_____

_____

_____

_____

In what areas do I need to put God on the throne of my life? How can I do this?

_____

_____

_____

_____

_____

Which areas of my life do I exhibit pride?

_____

_____

_____

_____

_____

Many a person, church and nation has seen its downfall and ruin because of pride. In what instances do I see the effects of pride in today's Church and our nation?

_____

_____

_____

_____

_____

Am I living as a child of the King or as king of the servants? What in my life supports this belief?

_____

_____

_____

_____

_____

Week 29
IT ONLY TAKES A FEW

*He will flatter and win over those who have
violated the covenant. But the people who know
their God will be strong and will resist him.*
- Daniel 11:32

The story is told in the book of Daniel about a small group of common folk who decided to take a stand against persecution and execution being committed by one of the most heinous men to ever walk this earth. In chapter 8 we read about Antiochus Epiphanes who ruled the Seleucid Empire. He was one of those few people throughout all of history who's ego was so inflated that he believed he was the 'god' all men should worship and because of this belief he was willing to do whatever it took to ensure all peoples did as he commanded. In fact, his self-given name of Epiphanes means 'god on earth'. However, because of his ruthless, toxic ways he was referred to as Antiochus Epimanes by the people which translated means the 'madman'.

As history demonstrates time and time again, it does not require large masses of people to stand for what is right, to redirect the course of history. On the contrary, most times great change has come at the hands of small groups, or even individuals, who have believed and transferred their beliefs into actions, realizing that what is happening is against God and thus needs to change. Here we find one of those times where if action had been spared, the outcome could have grown much worse. But because a few decided that the pursuit of God and His holiness was greater than life itself, these few were used to save many.

Antiochus had become so compelled in his pursuit to re-establish and resurrect the empire of Alexander the Great, as he marched from city to city throughout Egypt that it had brought him face to face with the Roman Empire. The Romans insisted that he halt his conquests, which drove him to complete rage and hostility. As history bears out Antiochus and his army would have been no match for Rome but this still did not slow down the ambitions of the maniacal tyrant. However, as unimaginable as it may seem, what may have ultimately prevented his complete demise at the hands of the Romans was an uprising in one of his provinces by the Jewish people. In fact, this enraged him deeper than the directive of Rome.

As we continue to learn, this event halted his return to Babylon and his, for certain, encounter with Rome as he instead proceeded to crush the uprising. As Antiochus and his army approached Jerusalem he gave his generals orders to utterly destroy the entire city and in doing so, they were to slaughter every Jew, whether young or old, male or female. This death and destruction was to run for 3 days straight and would take the lives of over 40,000 Jewish people, at which the end would simply be the beginning of persecution for those remaining.

After this Antiochus would capture and exile those remaining, abolish all rights and practices of religious freedom, have those who did not submit executed and would once again return to destroy the entire interior of the city. The only remnant left in place was that of the Temple and only for the sole reason of desecrating it and erecting himself as 'god'. It was now time for the few who would mount the insurrection! They would be used to not only restore the worship of the One True God but would also remove the heavy hand of this unhinged lunatic. Mattathias, an elderly Jewish priest, returned to his home in Modein and rallied a group to stand strong, refusing to bow to the false gods of Antiochus, and to take military action against the oppressors. It was now that the real test of their resolute would be faced.

Antiochus had sent a band of soldiers throughout the provinces attempting to force all people to worship who and how he had commanded. So when this contingent showed up at the door of Mattathias, the courageousness of a few would be on full display for all to see. Apelles commanded Mattathias to desecrate the commands of God or lose his life. Many, including a townsman, would easily set aside his beliefs for sake of his life, but not this man or his family.

Instead Mattathias and his sons took the fight to this evil

man and soldiers, bringing down all without losing one of their own. Immediately, Mattathias called for the townspeople to flee with him to the mountains. The people responded by leaving all behind, except for weapons and food. Word of their valor travelled quickly and soon many others were inspired to do likewise. Rather quickly Mattathias and his sons were able to build a formidable revolution which would ultimately deliver the Jewish people from the most atrocious despot that the nation of Israel had ever known, producing independence for the first time in over 400 years.

Now, after having read what a Jewish priest and his few countrymen were able to accomplish against an ominous threat and world power, why do we still think we can't be used today? Or that one person can't really make a difference? And yet whether we truly believe these lies or not, why do we live like we do? The fact is God does not need us to accomplish His will but He chooses us to be part of His plan. Even more, God does not need us to be the brightest, the strongest or the best leader; He simply calls us to be willing.

Today, stop waiting for someone else to step up and stand for God and let it begin with us. Just like the revolution that Mattathias was able to inspire, let us inspire a revolution of our own; one where we stop believing the lie that we're not worthy or talented enough and simply start taking God at His word. For as Paul said, *"Each time he said, 'My grace is all you need. My power works best in weakness.' So now I am glad to boast about my weaknesses, so that the power of Christ can work through me."* - II Cor. 12:9.

Food for Thought

The Bible says in II Timothy 2:21," *If you keep yourself pure, you will be a special utensil for honorable use. Your life will be clean, and you will be ready for the Master to use you for every good work.*" Am I clean and fit for the Master's use? If not, why? Since God desires to use me, how is that happening?

_____

_____

_____

_____

_____

_____

_____

List the ways I allow the enemy to make me think I can't do anything lasting.

_____

_____

_____

_____

_____

_____

_____

_____

Name the ways I can step outside my comfort zone and do something incredible for Christ.

_____

_____

_____

_____

_____

Cite 3 historical believers who have stood up for Christ endangering their own lives. How would they have the strength to do so? Do I?

_____

_____

_____

_____

_____

What can I do today to begin standing for Christ in a hostile political society? Be specific.

_____

_____

_____

_____

_____

✝

Week 30
THE MASTER'S RETURN

Later, Jesus sat on the Mount of Olives. His disciples
came to him privately and said, "Tell us, when will all
this happen? What sign will signal your return...?"
- Matthew 24:3

I can't recall when or how I heard the story of John, the chauffeur, but he used to work for a Christian who was a faithful witness for Christ whom God had richly blessed. Often the man of God would talk with John about his soul, the necessity of accepting Christ and being ready for what lay beyond this life. One day, while telling his driver of the blessed hope of the Lord's return, he said to him, *"John, when the Lord comes, you may have my cars."* This evoked from John a polite and very joyous expression of gratitude. *"And John,"* he added, *"you and your wife can come and live in our nice large house."* Again John responded with a very fervent *"Thank you, sir!"* He also told John that he could have all the money and property he possessed when the Lord Jesus came.

Thrilled, John returned to his home and told his wife what his boss had said. Both were elated at the prospect but had not considered the implications. John went to bed but could not sleep. In the middle of the night he made his way to his boss's house and knocked loudly till he came and asked who was there. *"It's me, John, your chauffeur"* was the reply from the other side of the locked door. *"What's the matter, John? Why have you come at this time of night?"* *"Oh sir"* said the chauffeur, *"I don't want your car."* *"Don't want my car, John? Why not?"* he asked. *"Nor your house, nor your money, nor your property,"* added John. *"Well, John, what is it that you do want?"* *"I want to be saved—to be ready, like you, for the coming of Jesus."*

In Matthew 24:37-42 Jesus said, *"When the Son of Man returns, it will be like it was in Noah's day. In those days before the flood, the people were enjoying banquets and parties and weddings right up to the time Noah entered his boat. People didn't realize what was going to happen until the flood came and swept them all away. That is the way it will be when the Son of Man comes. Two men will be working together in the field; one will be taken, the other left. Two women will be grinding flour at the mill; one will be taken, the other left. So you, too, must keep watch! For you don't know what day your Lord is coming."*

Jesus not only foretold of His death, burial and resurrection in great deal before it came to pass but He also foretold of His return to receive His own to a home in Heaven. In fact, as we read, Jesus foretold what the times would look like prior to His return but also warned man to be prepared as it would come as a great surprise to many. The events of today seem to point to the imminent return of Jesus, so the question everyone needs to have an answer to is, am I ready?

In John 14:1-3 Jesus told His disciples, *"Don't let your hearts be troubled. Trust in God, and trust also in me. There is more than enough room in my Father's home. If this were not so, would I have told you that I am going to prepare a place for you? When everything is ready, I will come and get you, so that you will always be with me where I am."* The fact is as Jesus came the first time to lay down His life for all, He is coming again to receive those who have placed their faith in Him.

Whether it be the race for nukes by North Korea, Iran and others; the constant barrage of attacks against Israel; the resurgence of the Russian empire; the domination of China as a global power; the rise of Islamic extremism; perpetual earthquakes and major storms; the ageless eroding of moral values; or the attack on Christian liberties, all of these signs and more point the way to the return of Christ.

While many argue that in spite of the tragedies unfolding, there is no sign of Christ's return. The reason for this also lies within what He told His disciples in John 14:3. As we recall, Jesus told them, *"When everything is ready, I will come and get you, so that you will always be with me where I am."* Well ask yourself, what constitutes readiness or what else must happen before He comes back? The answer is actually quite simple. He, King Jesus, is waiting for that last soul to come to the knowledge of His saving power and to accept Him as Lord and Savior of one's life. Jesus is extremely patient knowing that once He returns the door will then be closed on those who had the opportunity. In fact, we read in II Peter 3:9, *"The Lord isn't really being slow about his promise, as some people think. No, he is being patient for your sake. He does not want anyone to be destroyed, but wants everyone to repent."*

Jesus is coming again; are you ready? Let our prayer be as Dr. Horatius Bonar used to repeat, *"Perhaps today, Lord"*.

Food for Thought

Am I ready for Christ's return? Is my family? Are my friends? If not, what am I doing to change it?

_____

_____

_____

_____

_____

What occupies my time, effort and attention? What am I spending my time pursuing? Eternal value or temporal substance?

_____

_____

_____

_____

_____

What signs can I see in the news today that show Christ's imminent return?

_____

_____

_____

_____

_____

If today happens to be the day, what will I be caught doing? Would I be embarrassed in my daily routine if Christ returned? Why or why not?

_____

_____

_____

_____

_____

Does Christ's coming return scare or excite me? Both? Why? Explain.

_____

_____

_____

_____

_____

_____

✝

Week 31
THE TRUTH
WHISPERER

*And you will know the truth, and
the truth will set you free.*
- John 8:32

A fun-loving but oh so true story is told how during a trial, in a small Missouri town, the local prosecuting attorney called his first witness to the stand. The witness was a proper well-dressed elderly lady, the Grandmother type, well spoken and poised. She was sworn in, asked if she would tell the truth, the whole truth and nothing but the truth, on the Bible, so help her God.

The prosecuting attorney approached the woman and asked, *"Mrs. Jones, do you know me?"* She responded, *"Why, yes I do know you, Mr. Williams. I've known you since you were a young boy and frankly, you've been a big disappointment to me. You lie, cheat on your wife, manipulate people and talk badly about them behind their backs. You think you're a rising big shot when you haven't the sense to realize you never will amount to anything more than a two-bit paper-pushing shyster. Yes, I know you quite well."*

The lawyer was stunned. Not knowing what else to do, he pointed across the room and asked, *"Mrs. Jones, do you know the defense attorney?"*

She again replied, *"Why, yes, I do. I've known Mr. Bradley since he was a youngster, too. He's lazy, bigoted, has a bad drinking problem. The man can't build or keep a normal relationship with anyone and his law practice is one of the worst in the entire state. Not to mention he cheated on his wife with three different women. Yes, I know him."*

The defense attorney almost fainted. Laughter mixed with gasps, thundered throughout the courtroom and the audience was on the verge of chaos.

At this point, the judge brought the courtroom to silence, called both counselors to the bench, and in a very quiet voice said, *"If either of you morons asks her if she knows me, you're going to jail."*

If we were in the court that day, would we be comfortable with Mrs. Jones describing us? Do we have things that we wouldn't want anyone else to know about? Even more, if called to testify on behalf of ourselves or someone else, would we tell the truth regardless the consequences? While this is a humorous story, it also demonstrates what one would be willing to endure if attempting to share the truth.

The concept of truth today seems to be a moving target. In other words, truth changes based upon the situation or the individual involved. Whether it be Hillary Clinton distorting the truth under oath or Alex Rodriguez shifting blame of performance enhancement steroid usage, the truth oftentimes only seems to be applicable to the common man. But is truth really fluid? And should truth be levied the same for everyone?

Many people would agree that what is undeniably true is that if ever true, it must always be true. The problem is that many attempt to misconstrue or even deliberately alter the truth in order to advance their own purpose. This is not only the case in politics and sports but it has extreme relevance to the Word of God.

As far back as the Garden of Eden, Satan attempted to place a cloud of ambiguity over the truth God had shared with Adam and Eve. The serpent did not come right out and call God a liar; instead he attempted to muddy the waters but insinuating, *"Is that what God really meant?"* In other words, was the truth really the truth or could it change based upon circumstances? However disguised, when one questions the one articulating truth, they are calling him a liar. And when one alters the facts to protect or advance personal beliefs or concerns, he has painted himself a liar.

So as believers do we live a life of truth and honesty, believing and applying the ultimate Truth, or does truth change based upon our desires and opinions? The irony about today's standard of truth is that we are told there is no black and white, simply grey. This is otherwise known as moral relativism which can be described as the view that moral judgments are true or false only relative to some particular standpoint (for instance, that of a culture, historical period or personal experience) and that no standpoint is uniquely privileged/valued over all others. Additionally, many attempt to push truth aside through the argument of education; the argument, 'we once believed that but now that we have more (or new) information, we see that it really wasn't so.' Unfortunately for those who prescribe to this belief, it flies in the face of biblical truth. For instance, Noah Webster once noted, *"The Bible must be considered as the great source of all the truth by which men are to be guided in government as well as in all social transactions."*

Today's world is in dire straits; it is craving absolute truth and for the man or woman who will be willing to stand up and shout it from the rooftop regardless the backlash he may experience. The Church needs to stand rock solid on the truth of the gospel and refuse to back down and pull away. And that which is true, which once was accepted as truth, needs to be re-established as the truth it has always been. It is time for truth to no longer be whispered but to be bellowed!

Francis Schaeffer once remarked, *"Today not only in philosophy but in politics, government and individual morality, our generation sees solutions in terms of synthesis and not absolutes. When this happens, truth, as people have always thought of truth, has died."* Let us return to the truth of the Word where right is right and wrong is evil. Let us display truth in our lives and herald it to the lost. For only through sharing Truth will we win the lost and save the dying. It's time we stop apologizing for the truth of the Gospel and realize it's the saving blood to all who will accept.

Food for Thought

What is truth to me? Does truth change? Is there absolute Truth?

_____

_____

_____

_____

_____

What does scripture say about truth? Be specific.

_____

_____

_____

_____

How has society today rejected biblical truth?

_____

_____

_____

_____

_____

Do I stand for truth? How am I exhibiting truth?

_____

_____

_____

_____

_____

What happens biblically and historically when an individual
or society reject truth?

_____

_____

_____

_____

_____

Week 32
TRUE LOVE WINS

This is my commandment: Love each other in the same way I have loved you. There is no greater love than to lay down one's life for one's friends.
- John 15:12-13

On Friday, June 26, 2015, the U.S. Supreme Court decided to re-write the constitutional definition of marriage and in essence, create new legislation when they legalized homosexual marriage. That day the Obama administration decided to show their support for the decree and their contempt for God and all of those who opposed this depravity in their rejection of God's word by illuminating the White House in an array of rainbow colors, the symbol of homosexual rights. The term coined, *"Love Wins"*, became the battle cry for those who sought to further their own agenda of perversion and self-interest, forgetting or ignoring the true beginning and foundation of the phrase. Love does win but not because of a distorted context but because Christ was willing to display His love for mankind through His death, burial and resurrection.

True love is not based on self-indulgence or even a physical attraction; true love is purposefully putting others before oneself. In fact, the Bible refers to this word in the Greek as agape. *Your Father Loves You*, James Packer once wrote, *"The Greek word agape (love) seems to have been virtually a Christian invention -- a new word for a new thing (apart from about twenty occurrences in the Greek version of the Old Testament, it is almost non-existent before the New Testament). Agape draws its meaning directly from the revelation of God in Christ. It is not a form of natural affection, however, intense, but a supernatural fruit of the Spirit. It is a matter of will rather than feeling (for Christians must love even those they dislike). It is the basic element in Christ-likeness."*

As one considers the phrase, *"It is a matter of will rather than feeling"*, we see in Jesus' example of how He willed Himself to obey His Father and to give His life on behalf of man. If love was merely a feeling the ability to endure the pain, torment and eventual death for another one would not stand the test. Too often feelings change like the wind; therefore, they are not enough to express and demonstrate love in the toughest of times. Would we be willing to die for someone that we truly didn't love? True love is doing something for another that costs us everything, not doing something for ourselves that costs us nothing.

As we look deeper at the concept of true love and the cost that is paid, we need to consider Romans 5:6-8 where we read, *"When we were utterly helpless, Christ came at just the right time and died for us sinners. Now, most people would not be willing to die for an upright person, though someone might perhaps be willing to die for a person who is especially good. But God showed his great love for us by sending Christ to die for us while we were still sinners."* Love is giving everything for someone else with no expectation in return.

Let us consider, what is true love? Seeking one's own at the expense of another or giving up everything for another? C.S. Lewis wrote, *"Do not waste your time bothering whether you 'love' your neighbor act as if you did. As soon as we do this, we find one of the great secrets. When you are behaving as if you loved someone, you will presently come to love him. If you injure someone you dislike, you will find yourself disliking him more. If you do him a good turn, you will find yourself disliking him less."* Love truly wins when we realize it's about others and not ourselves.

As believers let us pray that we demonstrate the love of Christ daily. The busyness of life and the sin of this world can make even the most tender of hearts cold and hard; it can remove all desire to love in the face of adversity. Let us remember that love will only win when we allow ourselves to be laid upon the altar of sacrifice as Christ; for then others will hear what we are for and not simply what we are against. As God loved the world, so let us love through His eyes and with His heart remembering *"Whoever loves much, does much"* (Thomas a'Kempis).

Food for Thought

In a society where love seems to mean anything to anyone, what are the characteristics of true love?

_____

_____

_____

_____

_____

Does the concept of biblical marriage still hold true today or should homosexual marriage be legal because 'times have changed'? Explain.

_____

_____

_____

_____

_____

_____

_____

_____

_____

If marriage is dependent upon a person's individual belief, or even society's, are there any limitations or should people be allowed to marry anyone or anything based upon conscience? Explain.

_____

_____

_____

_____

_____

Jesus not only spoke about love, He showed it. What does the scripture say love ought to reflect?

_____

_____

_____

_____

Am I showing love to everyone? If not, who do I not love? How can I change the way I treat others to express Godly love?

_____

_____

_____

_____

✝

Week 33
DO WHAT MATTERS

So let's not get tired of doing what is good.
At just the right time we will reap a harvest
of blessing if we don't give up.
- Galatians 6:9

Years ago John W. Gardner, former Secretary of Health, Education and Welfare under President Johnson and founding chairman of Common Cause, said it was a rare and high privilege to help people understand the difference they can make -- not only in their own lives, but also in the lives of others, simply by giving of themselves.

Secretary Gardner tells of a cheerful old man who asked the same question of just about every new acquaintance he found himself in conversation with - *"What have you done that you believe in and you are proud of?"*, he would inquire.

He never asked typical questions such as, *"What do you do for a living?"* It was always, *"What have you done that you believe in and are proud of?"*

It was an unnerving question for people who had built their entire self-worth on their wealth or their family name or their exalted job title.

The old man did not think himself to be a fierce interrogator but was one day delighted by a woman who answered, *"I'm doing a good job raising three children;"* and by a cabinetmaker who said, *"I believe in good workmanship and practice it;"* and by a woman who said, *"I started a bookstore and it's the best bookstore for miles around."*

"I don't really care how they answer," said the old man. *"I just want to put the thought into their minds."*

"They should live their lives in such a way that they can have a good answer. Not a good answer for me, but for themselves. That's what's important."

The responsibilities of life can sometimes have us chasing our tails like a hamster on a pinwheel; every day simply trying to make ends meet. But at the end of our days will we be able to look back, reflecting on a life well lived, or will we have regrets for not having accomplished what mattered most? As believers we know that our life mission is to exalt the name of Christ through word and deed – so, how well are we living up to that calling? What is it that we deem important in our lives? Do we esteem the same things as God or does the matter of our life exist in the amount of matter that revolves around us?

A famous passage about chasing after what matters most in life is a story told about a conversation that Jesus had with an extremely rich man. In Mark 10 we read about how the rich man approached Jesus wanting to know what he needed to do to inherit eternal life. Upon Jesus' first response, the rich man's heart was lifted (if nothing else than in false hope) as he believed he had fulfilled all Jesus taught. But upon further discussion, Jesus' follow up instructions left this man walking away with great remorse as he saw Jesus' directives to be more than he could muster. In verses 20-25 we read, *"Teacher,"* the man replied, *"I've obeyed all these commandments since I was young."* Looking at the man, Jesus felt genuine love for him. *"There is still one thing you haven't done,"* he told him. *"Go and sell all your possessions and give the money to the poor, and you will have treasure in heaven. Then come, follow me."* At this the man's face fell, and he went away sad, for he had many possessions. Jesus looked around and said to his disciples, *"How hard it is for the rich to enter the Kingdom of God!"* This amazed them. But Jesus said again, *"Dear children, it is very hard to enter the Kingdom of God. In fact, it is easier for a camel to go through the eye of a needle than for a rich person to enter the Kingdom of God!"* According to Jesus what matters most in life can be summed up in the two great commandments – *"Love your God with all your heart, all your soul, all your mind and all your strength"* and *"Love your neighbor as yourself"*.

I was heard that news commentator Dan Rather had a good way of always keeping his professional objective in mind. He said he often looked at a question he'd written on three slips of paper. The first one he kept in his wallet, the second in his shirt pocket and the third, forever on his desk. The simple question asked, *"Is what you are doing now helping the broadcast?"* I believe as Christ-followers we ought to be asking ourselves, *"Is what I'm doing furthering the kingdom of Christ and helping others?"* - *"Does it matter?"* - And *"If not me, then who?"*

Life is all about choices. From the simple choices of, *"what will I eat for lunch?"* to the mid-level choices of, *"where will I choose to live?"* to the complex choices of, *"what will be the story of my life?"* In other words, will my life be summarized as one that mattered? Will it be seen as having made a difference? Or will it be highlighted as one of selfish desire for the here and now in lieu of laying hold on eternal value? As John Hagee once remarked, *"The measure of a man's greatness is not the number of servants he has, but the number of people he serves"*. We only have one life to live, let's make sure we spend it on the things that matter!

Food for Thought

List the top 3 things that matter to me in life. Be specific.

_____

_____

_____

_____

_____

Do my priorities align with Scripture? If not, what needs to change?

_____

_____

_____

_____

_____

The old expression says, *"A person wrapped up in themselves is an awful small package"*. Do I see life as an investment in others or am I more focused on withdrawals?

_____

_____

_____

_____

It has been noted that one never sees an armor truck following a hearse. At the end of my life will I look back and say, *"I should've spent more time at work or I should've spent more time with my family."* Am I living each day with the end in mind?

_____

_____

_____

_____

It can be noted that if an event or action won't change the outcome of life, it is irrelevant. So how do I stay focused on the important stuff of life?

_____

_____

_____

_____

_____

_____

_____

✝

Week 34
THEN THEY CAME FOR ME

Then the others grabbed Jesus
and arrested him.
- Matthew 26:50b

Martin Niemoller was a decorated U-boat captain in the First World War. Subsequently he became a distinguished Protestant pastor who would emerge as a straightforward speaking public adversary of Adolf Hitler as the Nazis increasingly gained a firm hold on the reins of power in Germany.

Niemoeller was an active leader in a so-called Pastors' Emergency League and in a Synod that denounced the abuses of the dictatorship in the famous *"Six Articles of Barmen."* Such actions finally led to his arrest on July 1, 1937. When the ensuing court appearance was followed by his release with only a modest 'slap on the wrist', Hitler personally ordered his imprisonment with the verdict that Niemoeller remain in a concentration camp, inclusive of long periods of solitary confinement, until the end of the war.

After the war, Niemoller occasionally traveled internationally and delivered many speeches and sermons in which he confessed his own blindness and inaction in earlier years when the Nazi regime rounded up the communists, socialists, trade unionists and, finally, the Jews.

His now famous quote signifies how as evil begins to attack, it will divide and drown out all who dare to challenge and if not opposed will eventually eradicate all. Niemoller penned the famous words, *"First they came for the Socialists, and I did not speak out—*

> *Because I was not a Socialist.*

> *Then they came for the Trade Unionists, and I did not speak out—*

> *Because I was not a Trade Unionist.*

> *Then they came for the Jews, and I did not speak out—*

> *Because I was not a Jew.*

> *Then they came for me—and there was no one left to speak for me."*

Today, the Church, like never since the book of Acts, is under such persecution. While many may not presently be experiencing such attacks, all one has to do is to turn on the television, read a newspaper or surf the web for current events and he will behold the atrocities occurring. However, since so many American believers are cushioned from the ills and barbarism transpiring around the world, we have chosen to remain silent and not become involved. In too many instances, only when such horrors begin to 'hit home' is it enough to lift one out of his apathy to become engaged; however, most times by this point, it is too late.

Similar to what transpired in Nazi Germany during WWII, Christians round the world and religious rights here at home are under extreme attack. So, as a believer, what can I be doing? First, believers need to be praying for each other. Whether it be family members, church members or believers in 'enemy territories' round the world. For any believer to not understand the assault being levied against brothers and sisters in Christ is unacceptable in today's digitalized world. All too often, those who claim no knowledge is not because it was unavailable but because it was not desired or sought after. In fact, the Bible tells us in Colossians 1:9 that we need to, *"So we have not stopped praying for you since we first heard about you"* and in Hebrews 4:16 we see, *"So let us come boldly to the throne of our gracious God. There we will receive his mercy, and we will find grace to help us when we need it most."* While we may not be able to house or provide material assistance and protection to the Saints in such places, every one of us can and should be praying for their protection and provision.

Next, we need to be about sharing the gospel with every one that we come into contact with. Many of us are familiar with passages like Matthew 28:18-20 often referred to as the Great

Commission and its counterpart found in Mark 16:15, but are we applying it or just acknowledging its existence? What about Acts 4:12 where we read, *"There is salvation in no one else! God has given no other name under heaven by which we must be saved."* So if Christ is the only way to heaven, then why do we refuse to confront and address the lies put forth from the pit of hell? As believers, as soldiers of the cross, it is incumbent we do not settle for political correctness over biblical accuracy.

Finally, as believers in a free society it is our obligation to oppose the daily blitz that threatens our liberties and the future of our nation. It is time that believers wake up and realize we are not yet in heaven – and since this is the case, it is paramount that we take an active role in our government and thus the policies and laws enacted. First and foremost, believers ought to pray for their national leaders. Both Romans 13:1-7 and Jeremiah 29:7 teach that a nation will be blessed or abased on the conduct of the believers within that land. We have the opportunity to bring God's blessing upon the remainder of our citizenry. Next, we are instructed to be a 'good citizen' that means with the most basic, yet important, of rights – voting. To be a good citizen and seek the blessing of God upon a nation, believers need to make their voice heard...while the door is open. Then there is the issue of national oppression, the erasure of Christian liberty and the decision of whom do I obey – God or man? For believers, there is no choice. As Peter noted in Acts 5:29, *"We must obey God rather than any human authority."* However, this requires great strength and boldness and often comes with terrible punishment and a possible death sentence.

So I ask, if one is unable to stand for Christ in a religious liberty abundant environment, how will he stand when the government comes against him? And if believers do not speak out when opportunity presents itself, while it is within their right, who will speak out when there is no one left? According to Chuck Colson, *"If Christians today understood this distinction between the role of the private Christian citizen and the Christian in government, they might sound less like medieval crusaders. If secularists understood correctly the nature of Christian public duty they would not fear, but welcome responsible Christian political involvement."*

If American believers continue to wallow with regard to their God-given citizenship responsibilities, America will cease to be the light on the mountain for the world. And if America is no longer there to speak on behalf of believers around the world, who will be there to speak on behalf of American Christians when they come for us? America is on the brink of simply becoming a once upon a time great nation in history. Now is the time for us to draw before God and cry out for ourselves and others while His mercy yet endures; otherwise we will become as *"Europe which has become a post-Christian culture in which the principal religious influence is visible in art treasures and cathedrals filled with tourists rather than worshipers"* (Chuck Colson).

Food for Thought

In a society where 'Good Samaritanship" is a lost art, do I speak on behalf of others or do I turn my head and avoid it if I don't think it will affect me?

_____

_____

_____

_____

_____

What does my prayer/faith life look like in regard to praying for brothers/sisters in Christ I have never met?

_____

_____

_____

_____

At what point does life become so devalued that I need to fear my own? If I was facing persecution, who would speak for me?

_____

_____

_____

_____

Christians are instructed to be good national citizens. How can I, as a Christian, affect my 'sphere of influence' to uphold biblical values in society?

_____

_____

_____

_____

_____

If believers continue to remain silent, in the corner of life, America will cease to be the Christian Nation God established. Therefore, if I'm not speaking for Christ now, how will I ever be able under oppression?

_____

_____

_____

_____

_____

✝

PESKY PEAS

And give thanks for everything to God the Father in the name of our Lord Jesus Christ.
- Ephesians 5:20

In the 1835 fairy tale, The Princess and the Pea, by Hans Christian Anderson, the story is told about a prince in search of his princess. The story unfolds as the young prince is unable to find his perfect mate; all prospective candidates being either too short or too tall, too fat or too thin, without the appropriate table manners or simply not attractive enough. There was never any pleasing of this young man. Then one rainy night low and behold a knock on the door of the castle would unite this prince with his heart's desire.

As the kingdom's guards answered the knock, a young girl stood before them, drenched to the bone, seeking a place of safety and comfort for the night. As she entered and was greeted by the queen, she told the story of her regal ancestry and posh position as a princess. The queen, not fully convinced by this stranger, would attempt to test and prove the truthfulness of her claim.

Upon welcoming her in, the queen instructed the chambermaids to place a pea in the bed, covered by 20 mattresses and another 20 feather-beds. Upon waking in the morning, the self-professed princess would fuss about how she never slept a wink because of the uncomfortableness of the bed. While she was upset over the situation, the prince leaped for joy, expressing how only a true princess would be so sensitive as to detect the tiniest imposition within the bed.

Even though she had been let in out of the rain; even though she had been dressed in the most splendor of clothing; even though she had been given the plushest of bedding to lie on, she still managed to find the smallest of nuisances to snivel about and drive her to grumbling. How often do we resemble this young princess? With all that God has given us, do we still whine and bellyache about what we don't have? Are we thankful for being given a warm, dry, safe place to dwell or do we gripe about the pea that we perceive as the obstruction to our comfort?

Saint Ignatius once noted, *"In the light of the Divine Goodness, it seems to me, though others may think differently, that ingratitude is the most abominable of sins and that it should be detested in the sight of our Creator and Lord by all of His creatures who are capable of enjoying His divine and everlasting glory."* What better example can be seen than the through the life of the nation of Israel. Over and over God would bless His people with Divine acts of goodness, only to see them turn up their nose in disgust. Whether it was a rain shower of manna from Heaven in the wilderness, or a promised land *"flowing with milk and honey"*, or the actual incarnation of God Himself in Jesus Christ, these people always found a reason to be unsatisfied. That is the ironic thing about lacking thankfulness; people become so ingrained in it they don't even realize it's happening. Regardless, God referred to His people as an *"evil congregation"*.

We could easily find ourselves rebuking the children of Israel for their ingratitude. I mean, who could possibly complain when being fed the bread of heaven? Or who could deny the miracles and victories played out in front of them and still find reason to doubt? And who would reject God Almighty in human form simply because He didn't meet their expectations? Yet we are just as guilty. Every day we complain, we express jealousy and we fail to thank God for His enduring mercies and blessings to us.

In the previous fairy tale, it may be a royal characteristic to notice the simplest and smallest annoyances, but in real life, constantly looking for what is wrong or not to our exact liking is simply self-centered and unappreciative. In fact, the Bible teaches in I Thessalonians 5:18, *"Be thankful in all circumstances,"* and in Ephesians 5:20, *"And give thanks for everything to God the Father in the name of our Lord Jesus Christ."* The heart and life of the contented is entrenched in a spirit of gratitude not displeasure. As Henry Ward Beecher concluded, *"The unthankful heart discovers no mercies; but let the thankful heart sweep through the day and as the magnet finds the iron, so it will find, in every hour, some heavenly blessings!"*

Today's Church is, on many plains, a mirror reflection of the Old Testament nation of Israel. As Americans we are blessed with wealth beyond compare. Even the poorest of American believers are wealthier than the richest of other nations – yet somehow we manage to focus on what we don't have and yet believe we should, instead of focusing on the daily blessings from God's eternal hand. As the Israelites spurned the heavenly provisions, we too often fail to appreciate the outpouring of God's storehouse in our lives. The spirit of ingratitude has become so engrained in society that it has managed to leak into the believers' lives. While on the other hand, if we change our perspective to a mindset of seeing the blessing in each day, each moment and each opportunity then we can say as did William Arthur Ward when he said, *"Gratitude can transform common days into thanksgivings, turn routine jobs into joy, and change ordinary opportunities into blessings."*

Food for Thought

America possesses more wealth than 90% of the world. Yet, Americans are some of the most ungrateful people in the world. Am I grateful for all of I have or do I complain about what I don't?

_____

_____

_____

_____

_____

_____

The Bible tells us in I Thessalonians 5:18, *"Be thankful in all circumstances"* and Ephesians 5:20 says, *"And give thanks for everything to God the Father in the name of our Lord Jesus Christ."* As a believer, do I thank God for everything (good and bad) that takes place in my life? Explain.

_____

_____

_____

_____

_____

_____

The Bible teaches in Philippians 2:14, *"Do everything without complaining and arguing."* Have I allowed an ungrateful generation and society to cause me to 'grumble' about life? Why or why not?

_____

_____

_____

_____

_____

Christ said in John 10:10, *"My purpose is to give them a rich and satisfying life."* Part of living an abundant life is finding contentment and joy in life. Am I living an 'abundant' life?

_____

_____

_____

_____

_____

Does the pea in my bed or pebble in my shoe ruin my entire mood? Is my joy founded on comfort and leisure or in Christ my Lord? Explain.

_____

_____

_____

_____

_____

✝

Week 36
STONES OF REMEMBRANCE

We will use these stones to build a memorial. In the future your children will ask you, "What do these stones mean?" Then you can tell them, "They remind us that the Jordan River stopped flowing when the Ark of the Lord's Covenant went across." These stones will stand as a memorial among the people of Israel forever.
- Joshua 4:6-7

One of our country's most famous articles declares, *"Four score and seven years ago our fathers brought forth, upon this continent, a new nation, conceived in Liberty, and dedicated to the proposition that all men are created equal.*

Now we are engaged in a great civil war, testing whether that nation, or any nation so conceived, and so dedicated, can long endure. We are met here on a great battlefield of that war. We have come to dedicate a portion of it as a final resting place for those who here gave their lives that that nation might live. It is altogether fitting and proper that we should do this.

But in a larger sense we cannot dedicate – we cannot consecrate – we cannot hallow this ground. The brave men, living and dead, who struggled, here, have consecrated it far above our poor power to add or detract. The world will little note, nor long remember, what we say here, but can never forget what they did here.

It is for us, the living, rather to be dedicated here to the unfinished work which they have, thus far, so nobly carried on. It is rather for us to be here dedicated to the great task remaining before us – that from these honored dead we take increased devotion to that cause for which they here gave the last full measure of devotion – that we here highly resolve that these dead shall not have died in vain; that this nation shall have a new birth of freedom; and that this government of the people, by the people, for the people, shall not perish from the earth."

Extremely powerful words that have echoed the halls of history. Words that eulogized the many whose blood was poured out of lives laid down. Words that depicted a torn and battered American Republic. Words which memorialized the actions exhibited over the course of four years, countless miles marched and the thousands who died from combat, starvation and disease; whose final destination would bring all who mourned and observed to Gettysburg, Pennsylvania.

Gettysburg is a truly historical memorial of a time gone by in which these great United States endured conflict, disharmony and blood-stained fields. The fields, the monument, and even Lincoln's speech serve as a reminder to all of the greatest internal conflict our nation has ever known. However, not only does Gettysburg remind us of our past but the words spoken on that solemn day helped to paint the direction our great nation would chart in order to reestablish peace, solidarity and unity moving forward.

Memorials are extremely important - for if we ever forget where we've come from or what has made us who we are then we are bound to repeat the same mistakes. However, memorials should also serve as well-springs of hope, reminders of God's grace and a call to a brighter future. Whether it be in the articulation of Joshua when he pronounced, *"They remind us that the Jordan River stopped flowing when the Ark of the Lord's Covenant went across. These stones will stand as a memorial among the people of Israel forever"* or when Lincoln declared, *"It is rather for us to be here dedicated to the great task remaining before us - that from these honored dead we take increased devotion to that cause for which they here gave the last full measure of devotion - that we here highly resolve that these dead shall not have died in vain; that this nation shall have a new birth of freedom; and that this government of the people, by the people, for the people, shall not perish from the earth"*, the memorials built and the lasting words of courage, inspiration and devotion help to steer a future path of victory not just a flashback to hardship. On both occasions, God chose a man who would reflect on the past but also look forward to the future. And it can also be noted regarding both instances that great leaders are not made in the absence of great pain but in the heart of it.

While we are able to visit places that serve as memorials, whether it be national parks, cemeteries or personal dwellings, memorials can also be expressed through actions and practices. The Lord Jesus left us a memorial in which to remember Himself but also as a future event to anticipate and look forward to through the Lord's Supper. In this memorial we are able to remember what Christ did for us on the cross of Calvary but also to look forward to the hope of His return. In fact, from the perspective of remembering this event and looking forward to the future, Christ said, *"Mark my words—I will not drink wine again until the day I drink it new with you in my Father's Kingdom."* - Matthew 26:29. Here we are able to view the memorial of the Lord's Supper from the perspective of saving grace but also as anticipation to our eternal home in Heaven.

Memorials can be uplifting or they can be discouraging – it all depends on what we choose to focus on and what we are willing to take away.

To every generation it is imperative that we are able to remember the past but from each generation there need to be those who will lift high the hope of the future. Memorials can be uplifting or they can be discouraging – it all depends on what we choose to focus on and what we are willing to take away. Let us remember all that God has done for us through the boulders in our lives but at the same time let us not sit back and think that's all there is; as long as we have a today, God has a plan.

Food for Thought

What faith memorials do I have to reflect upon regarding Christ's provision and protection in my life? Be specific.

_____

_____

_____

_____

_____

As memorials are great to look back on as a reminder of God's goodness, am I caught only looking in the rear view mirror or am I using it as the impetus to move forward in faith? Explain.

_____

_____

_____

_____

_____

Am I reminding others of God's blessings or am I causing others to stumble? How?

_____

_____

_____

_____

_____

What will future generations have to say about me when they look back on my faith life? Will it encourage and challenge or will I be another name in history? Explain.

_____

_____

_____

_____

_____

_____

When I celebrate the Lord's Supper do I recognize it as a memorial of the past but also as a reminder of my future? How does that understanding affect the way I live?

_____

_____

_____

_____

_____

_____

✝

Week 37
PRAISING GOD
IN THE PIT

*He lifted me out of the pit of despair, out of
the mud and the mire. He set my feet on solid
ground and steadied me as I walked along.*
- Psalm 40:2

Imagine what disdain and even hatred one must have for another to toss him in a pit in an attempt to bury him alive. This is the experience that Joseph endured at the hands of his brothers. The pot of contention had been boiling for quite some time between the siblings as Joseph upon the revelation of each dream proceeded to share it. In fact, Joseph's dreams pointed to a time where his brothers would bow before him. Remember, there was already a divide between Joseph and his older brothers due to the partiality that their father, Jacob, outwardly demonstrated. So when the opportunity availed itself for the brothers to rid themselves of Joseph, out of the jealousy and disgust harbored deep in their hearts, they decided to make the move.

The Bible tells us in Genesis 37:18-20 how, *"When Joseph's brothers saw him coming, they recognized him in the distance. As he approached, they made plans to kill him. 'Here comes the dreamer!'"* they said. *"Come on, let's kill him and throw him into one of these pits. We can tell our father, 'A wild animal has eaten him.' Then we'll see what becomes of his dreams!"* Hatred can compel anyone to do the inconceivable to even those closet of heart for the advancement of their own selfish desires.

As Joseph approached and his brothers conspired how they would bring about his demise, Reuben spoke up, *"Let's not kill him, why should we shed any blood? Let's just throw him into this empty pit here in the wilderness. Then he'll die without our laying a hand on him"* - Gen. 37:21-22; ultimately planning to return and free him. So the brothers agreed and as Joseph came upon them, *"they grabbed him and threw him into the pit, for the pit was empty."* - Gen. 37:24. While things certainly looked disheartening, blood-curdling and even terminal for Joseph, the brothers happened upon a band of Ishmaelite traders. *"Wow!"* they must have thought. *"Now we can not only get rid of him but we can make an easy buck as well."* So they sold him and swore allegiance to each other how they would take this action to their graves.

The feelings that Joseph must have been confronted with during these few hours are unimaginable – from anxiety and fear of how or when he would die to what would become of his father and little brother, Benjamin to what must have I done for my brothers to hate me so much. While all of these thoughts would most certainly have been understandable, the

Bible does not record any of them. However, what the Bible does tell us is that Joseph *"succeeded in everything he did as he served in the home of his Egyptian master."* - Gen. 39:2. So we need to ask ourselves, why? What did Joseph do while in the pit that would lead to a prosperous and influential position just a short time down the road? How could Joseph have trusted and even praised God in the pit when he was uncertain whether it might be the end? These are the lessons that we all need to learn - for we will all find ourselves in a 'pit' at some point in life.

While we don't know exactly what occurred during those moments Joseph lay in the pit, one can reasonably argue that he, as did the Psalmist, may have voiced the words, *"I waited patiently for the Lord to help me, and he turned to me and heard my cry. He lifted me out of the pit of despair, out of the mud and the mire. He set my feet on solid ground and steadied me as I walked along. He has given me a new song to sing, a hymn of praise to our God. Many will see what he has done and be amazed. They will put their trust in the Lord"* - Psalm 40:1-3. Looking back one can contend that the pit, not the dreams, are what made Joseph. For in these moments he learned like Corrie Ten Boom, *"You can never learn that Christ is all you need, until Christ is all you have."*

As people and as believers there will be moments in life that we find ourselves in the pit. However, what we choose to do while in the pit is what will make or break our life when we get out. Will we praise God in the pit or will we curse God for the pit? May we be able to proclaim,

"Lord, I've never moved a mountain and I guess I never will. All the faith that I could muster wouldn't move a small ant hill. Yet I'll tell you, Lord, I'm grateful for the joy of knowing Thee, and for all the mountain moving down through life You've done for me.

When I needed some help you lifted me from the depths of great despair. And when burdens, pain and sorrow have been more than I can bear, you have always been my courage to restore life's troubled sea, and to move these little mountains that have looked so big to me.

Many times when I've had problems and when bills I've had to pay, and the worries and the heartaches just kept mounting every day, Lord, I don't know how you did it. Can't explain the wheres or whys. All I know, I've seen these mountains turn to blessings in disguise.

No, I've never moved a mountain, for my faith is far too small. Yet, I thank you, Lord of Heaven, you have always heard my call. And as long as there are mountains in my life, I'll have no fear, for the mountain-moving Jesus is my strength and always near."

Food for Thought

Do I allow others feelings, attitudes or opinions to alter the way I live? How?

_____

_____

_____

_____

_____

Am I fearful to share God's words for fear of retribution?

_____

_____

_____

_____

How can I become more resilient and brazen in sharing God's word?

_____

_____

_____

_____

When difficulties arise, do I fear the depth of the pit or do I use it as an opportunity to praise God? Explain.

_____

_____

_____

_____

_____

_____

How do I expect my faith to be strengthened if I am unable to endure the struggles?

_____

_____

_____

_____

_____

_____

✝

Week 38
SINCERE FAITH

*I remember your genuine faith, for you share
the faith that first filled your grandmother
Lois and your mother, Eunice. And I know
that same faith continues strong in you.*
- II Timothy 1:5

A missionary once told the story of how a poor ungodly woman came to know Christ and her remarkable simple faith. Upon accepting Christ, she took Him literally at His word. Some months after her salvation her little boy became sick. His recovery was doubtful. Ice was needed for the little one, but in her tropical country, away from the great cities, it was so hard to come by. *"I'm going to ask God to send ice,"* the mother said to the missionary. *"Oh, but you can't expect that He will do that,"* was the quick reply. *"Why not?"* asked the simple-hearted believer. *"He has all the power, and He loves us. You told us so. I shall ask Him, and I believe He will send it."* She did ask Him, and God answered. Soon there came up a heavy thunder storm, accompanied by hail. The woman was able to gather a large bowlful of hailstones. The cold application was just what was needed, and the child recovered.

Sincerity can mark the difference between answered prayers and a solid foundational Christian life or a life that is filled with fear, anxiety and doubt. The dictionary defines sincere as, *"free from pretense or deceit; proceeding from genuine feelings"*. In other words, when one is sincere, he is honest and committed to his word or belief. Thus sincere faith is faith that is wholly centered on truth and attempts to avoid deceit or personal gain.

As Paul addressed young Timothy he commended him for his family tree which represented generations of sincere faith in Christ. Faith that was reproduced in others; faith that remained strong even in the face of adversity; and faith that would produce fruit beyond his lifetime. And even though Timothy was attacked with doubts of inferiority or inadequacy, his faith endured, abided and grew stronger because of the sincerity of his heart. God did not choose Timothy because of his attributes or talents, but because He knew of Timothy's sincere and devoted love for Him. Charles Spurgeon once described it as, *"Sincerity makes the very least person to be of more value than the most talented hypocrite."*

However, sincerity of itself will not strengthen one's faith or even produce genuine faith. Many people are sincere in their method of faith but they are also sincerely wrong. The basis of one's faith is more important than the sincerity of it. In fact, Anthony Farindon, a famous English preacher in the early 1600's, once asserted, *"Talk what we will of faith, if we do not trust and rely upon Him, we do not believe in Him."* Paul was not simply just applauding Timothy for his dedication to a cause but for his candor and for the truth of the Gospel founded upon Jesus Christ the cornerstone of genuine faith.

As believers today, how does the earnestness of our faith stack up to those of old, and most importantly, to the Word of God? Does our faith reflect a frankness and veracity or are we simply going through the motions? Is our faith centered on Christ and serving Him in all we do or is our faith contingent upon feelings, circumstances and people? Many attempt to use the excuse, *"I don't attend church because it's filled with hypocrites"*; however, that begs the question as to why one is attending church for others and not God alone? Faith – sincere faith predicated on Christ – a genuine faith established in God alone – is a faith that will carry one through the valleys as well as keeping his feet grounded on the mountaintops; will sustain one in the darkest storms of life; and will fetch one from the pits of a hell-spent future and fix his feet on the Rock of salvation.

Many a believer today faces a predicament between sincere faith and a contemporary faith – that is, a faith that simply shifts with the tides of generational philosophies. A. W. Tozer declared, *"Christianity is decaying and going down into the gutter because the God of modern Christianity is not the God of the Bible."* Realizing that Tozer died in 1963 and was simply beginning to see the onset of such liberal and progressive tenants, it is hard to imagine what he would think of the Church today?

Present day Christian faith is not a faith found in and dependent wholly upon God, it has become a value system that attempts to plug God in where we are comfortable for Him to dwell. Man, even believers, have become so comfortable in this world that sincerity in anything, yet alone Christ-like faith and dependence, has become virtually drowned out. Sincere faith, the original and foundational faith of the scriptures, calls us to live as if we have no other recourse for the salvation of our soul – for in reality, we do not. Francis Chan once noted, *"God doesn't call us to be comfortable. He calls us to trust Him so completely that we are unafraid to put ourselves in situations where we will be in trouble if He doesn't come through."* Paul was not comfortable. Timothy was not comfortable. Timothy's mother and grandmother were not comfortable in their faith. In fact, they lived in the exact opposite of comfort as unwanted inhabitants of a foreign land. As believers, are we not also inhabitants of a foreign world? Then why is it that we seem more concerned with being welcomed and accepted than being known as believers with a sincere faith in Christ?

Sincerity is the opposite of fraudulent; so the question we must ask ourselves is, 'Are we sincere (real, genuine and authentic) believers or are we simply frauds (fakes, imposters and hypocrites)?' In a day where it is clearly evident that our Savior's return is at hand, what will be said of us upon His return? Prayerfully He will not say to us, *"So why do you keep calling me 'Lord, Lord!' when you don't do what I say?"* - Luke 6:46. The world is looking for genuineness of action before they are willing to listen to the grandest of eloquent, verbose words. Let us be known as simple men, having a sincere faith that is sincerely rooted in Jesus Christ.

Food for Thought

As a person, is my faith sincerely founded upon Christ or am I sincerely wrong in my approach?

_____

_____

_____

_____

_____

Do I rely upon Christ working through me for my welfare or am I relying upon my own perceived strengths and talents?

_____

_____

_____

_____

_____

How do my actions, the way I live, demonstrate my faith and conviction in God's word? Be specific.

_____

_____

_____

_____

_____

Have I allowed the philosophy of 'contemporary Christianity' to diffuse the faith and Christianity of the Bible in my life? Explain.

_____

_____

_____

_____

_____

_____

_____

When my time has ended, will it be said of me as it was of Timothy's mother and grandmother, that I had left a lasting Christian legacy in my family or will I have simply been another person with no impact in history? What can I do to change that today?

_____

_____

_____

_____

_____

_____

_____

✝

Week 39
CHAIN BREAKER

The night before Peter was to be placed on trial, he was asleep, fastened with two chains between two soldiers. Others stood guard at the prison gate. Suddenly, there was a bright light in the cell, and an angel of the Lord stood before Peter. The angel struck him on the side to awaken him and said, "Quick! Get up!" And the chains fell off his wrists.
- Acts 12:6-7

It was a dark and lonely night as Peter sat in prison. By order of King Herod Agrippa, Peter had been arrested and placed in prison to await execution. By all apparent circumstances, the outlook for Peter did not fare well. One of his oldest friends, James (John's brother), had recently been put to death and now it would appear Peter was to be next.

However, in a nearby part of town, just a few blocks away, fellow believers gathered together in earnest prayer for his release and pardon. Yes, the Church was demonstrating one of its primary roles in that it was praying for its own. In Ephesians 6:18 we read, *"Praying at all times in the Spirit, with all prayer and supplication. To that end keep alert with all perseverance, making supplication for all the saints,"* Believers from near and far had gathered together on their knees and were beseeching God's miraculous intervention in a situation that was beyond the control or influence of any man. If God did not interject Himself, Peter's life would most certainly come to the end.

As the hours passed by, while the Church prayed, Peter laid down and went to sleep. Whether in peace knowing that God's will would be served either way or perhaps simply exhausted physically, emotionally and spiritually, Peter could no longer keep his eyes open. In the deep, dark hours of late night or early morning hours, God would once again answer the prayers of His people and bring relief and safety to His man.

"Peter, wake up!" are the words he heard as the angel of the Lord stood by his side shaking him. Who is to know whether at first Peter believed he was dreaming or whether he was so groggy that he had no idea what was taking place. Either way, as Peter awakened his chains fell off. At that moment, God, through use of His angel, transported Peter from the belly of a dungeon to the outside of the city walls where Peter would be able to make his way to the house of his fellow believers, seeking the face of God.

In those darkest, frightening hours of uncertainty and persecution, when no man could rescue or bring peace, God broke the chains that imprisoned Peter. The chains of bondage that held him down and held him back were the very same chains that God demonstrated His power over. And while we may never know if God would have still delivered Peter had the Church not come together to lift him up, in the end, God showed up and He showed off, revealing his power and authority over the temporal world and the spiritual world alike.

Accessing, claiming and implementing the power of the mighty Chain Breaker is available to all. However, while God can remove chains and restore victory, He also requires that we lay aside ourselves and seek Him to the utmost. Just as the local believers sought God on behalf of Peter, we need to be seeking God's deliverance for ourselves and for others from the bondage induced by the chains of sin and circumstances. In fact, Joyce Meyer once noted it as, *"God wants you to be delivered from what you have done and from what has been done to you – Both are equally important to Him."*

Chains can make one feel like they are drowning – and the anxiety produced can make it seem impossible to even breathe. Oftentimes, chains can even seem permanent and indestructible. Whether the chain is relational, situational or circumstantial, it can frequently make one feel caged and subdued. Even though Peter was an Apostle of Christ and even though the local body of believers were huddled in prayer for his freedom, to both, the chains may have seemed irreversible and impenetrable. Otherwise, why would the Church have demonstrated a sense of amazement at his presence with the response, *"You're out of your mind!"* they said. When she insisted, they decided, *"It must be his angel."* Even those who seem to have the godliest of relationships or the strongest prayer life can at times be overcome with chains of doubt, chains of unbelief or chains of hesitation.

In order for the chains that grip our lives to be broken asunder, we need to ensure that we engage the 'Chain Splitter'. Prayer is essential to a release from the chains that bind us, that grip us and entrap us; but faith in prayer and in the One whom the prayer is sent is critical. Paul exhorts us in Hebrews 11:6, *"And it is impossible to please God without faith. Anyone who wants to come to him must believe that God exists and that he rewards those who sincerely seek him."* As Thomas Watson once said, *"The angel fetched Peter out of the prison, but it was prayer that fetched the angel."*

Today you may be facing chains of imprisonment in your life; chains that seem strong and unbreakable; chains that have prevented victory; or chains that present a perception of demise and ruin. And like Peter, unless God miraculously intervenes, there will be no escape. However, praise God that He is the mighty Chain Breaker! Instead of going down to the local hardware store in a vain attempt to remove the chains, new or old, cry out to the Heavenly Locksmith and ask Him to smash the chains clutching your life. May you as Peter be able to exclaim upon freedom from the chains that bind, *"It's really true!"* *"It's really true!"*

Food for Thought

What specific chains are holding me down today?

_____

_____

_____

_____

_____

In the midst of the chains, do I still believe Christ is reigning on the throne? Why aren't I living like it?

_____

_____

_____

_____

One can easily become discouraged with the trends of today. Am I using the struggles in life to further the Kingdom or am I detracting from it?

_____

_____

_____

_____

Am I living as if God is still God in the bad times and well as the good times? Provide examples.

_____

_____

_____

_____

_____

_____

If I was to be in God's eternal presence today, would He find me faithful and sure or would I be embarrassed for fear and doubt? Explain.

_____

_____

_____

_____

_____

_____

✝

Week 40
CORNERSTONE

Therefore, this is what the Sovereign Lord says: "Look! I am placing a foundation stone in Jerusalem, a firm and tested stone. It is a precious cornerstone that is safe to build on. Whoever believes need never be shaken."
- Isaiah 28:16

I once heard a story how back when the Old West was being settled, pioneers flocked across the country to California and Oregon. In one particular spot on the Eastern slopes of the Rockies there was a large, dirt covered rock protruding in the middle of the trail. Wagon wheels were broken on it and men tripped over it. Finally, someone dug up the odd stone and rolled it off the trail into a nearby stream. The stream was too wide to jump over so people quickly began using the stone as a step to cross the cold creek. It was used for years, until finally one settler built his cabin near the stream. He moved the odd stone out of the stream and placed it in his cabin to serve as a doorstop.

As years passed, railroads were built and towns sprang up. The old settler's grandson went east to study geology. On a visit to his grandfather's cabin, the grandson happened to examine the old lump of stone and discovered within that lump of dirt and rock was the largest pure gold nugget ever discovered on the Eastern slope of the Rockies. It had been there for three generations and people never recognized its value. To some it was a stumbling stone to be removed. To others it was a stepping-stone, and to others it was just a heavy rock. But only the grandson saw it for what it really was!

The concept of the cornerstone originates from the first stone set in the construction of a masonry foundation, important since all other stones will be set in sequence to this stone, hence determining the direction and durability of the entire structure. Biblically the term cornerstone is prophesied in the Old Testament and fulfilled in the New Testament through Jesus Christ who is the chief cornerstone; whereas the apostles and prophets are foundation stones, and the whole building, or the church, is the holy temple built on the Lord. Furthermore, the stone laid in Zion, described in Isaiah 28:16, *"Therefore, this is what the Sovereign Lord says: 'Look! I am placing a foundation stone in Jerusalem, a firm and tested stone. It is a precious cornerstone that is safe to build on. Whoever believes need never be shaken'"* signals the precious value of said stone to the believer; but as the stone placed at the *"head of the corner"*, that is exalted, as in Psalm 118:22, *"The stone that the builders rejected has now become the cornerstone"*, He is a stone of offense and stumbling to those who refuse to believe. The metaphor describes well how the cornerstone is either a source of blessing or judgment,

Page 262

depending on a person's attitude toward it.

So the question we all need to ask ourselves is, *"What are we building our lives on?"* Do we have a solid foundation built on the everlasting Rock of ages or are we attempting to build our lives on our own merits which will end in quick, sinking sand? Jesus gave an analogy in Matthew 7:24-27 when He said, *"Anyone who listens to my teaching and follows it is wise, like a person who builds a house on solid rock. Though the rain comes in torrents and the floodwaters rise and the winds beat against that house, it won't collapse because it is built on bedrock. But anyone who hears my teaching and doesn't obey it is foolish, like a person who builds a house on sand. When the rains and floods come and the winds beat against that house, it will collapse with a mighty crash."*

Two primary lessons that can be learned from this text are (1) the eternal aspect and (2) the temporal/physical aspect. With respect to the eternal aspect, as we have previously learned, Jesus is the cornerstone for all of life. He is the building block for the Church, but more specifically, the individual. A person who places his trust in Him will hence be afforded forgiveness of sin, eternal life, and a home in Heaven in the loving presence of God Almighty. But at the same time, we also learned that the cornerstone (Jesus) will be a stumbling block to those who don't believe. In other words, rejection of the cornerstone will result in eternal damnation.

Secondly for the believer, building one's life upon the cornerstone will provide security and consistency; security in knowing regardless what storms of life may come our way, Christ will be there to provide peace and protection; consistency in the fact that our lives will not be as a roller coaster, constantly roaring up one minute and down the next. While it is possible for one to build his eternal prospect on the cornerstone it is also quite common for the same man to build his temporal on his own pebble. For this individual their eternal estate is not in question but how rocky the road will be is something that leaves many a man tossed to and fro. As Charles Stanley has commented, *"If we have built on the fragile cornerstones of human wisdom, pride and conditional love, things may look good for a while, but a weak foundation causes collapse when storms hit."*

From someone who has spent time working construction and laying foundations, I understand how important that first block will be; it feeds the balance and direction of every proceeding block. Now considering how important a concrete block is in forming the foundation for a house, an office building, a hotel and every other architectural structure, how much more important is it that we build our lives on a solid rock that will not falter? Jesus is the cornerstone to the stability and steadfastness needed in life. He is the One to build all of life's components on. As Charles Stanley concluded, *"There is only one secure foundation: a genuine, deep relationship with Jesus Christ, which will carry you through any and all turmoil."*

Food for Thought

What is the cornerstone of my life? Is it Christ or myself? Explain.

_____

_____

_____

_____

_____

Does my church treat Christ as the cornerstone or has He become an afterthought? Explain.

_____

_____

_____

_____

_____

While I may view Christ as my anchor for eternal security, am I attempting to live this life on my own?

_____

_____

_____

_____

_____

Many folks evaluate their success on status or possessions, what am I living my life for?

_____

_____

_____

_____

_____

_____

Is my foundation straight and secure, or is it shifty and weak? Is it solid in all 'weather patterns' or does it move when the 'weather' changes?

_____

_____

_____

_____

_____

_____

Week 41
EXCEPT I SEE

But he replied, "I won't believe it unless I see the nail wounds in his hands, put my fingers into them, and place my hand into the wound in his side."
- John 20:25b

As the preacher began his sermon he told the story of how a man read an ad in the newspaper, *"Hunting dog for sale, $5,000.00, but well worth it."* Being intrigued, he immediately called the number and the man told him that he had to see the dog in action. Early, the very next morning, they met and went hunting. The dog raced through the field and flushed two birds from a clump of bushes. The men fired and the birds fell into the water. It was now time for the miracle dog to go into action. He bounded on top of the water, grabbed the birds, and simply strutted back, the same way he had gone, on top of the water. The man was amazed to say the least and bought the dog on the spot. The next day he persuaded his brother to go hunting with him. They flushed a couple of birds and the dog again leaped on top of the water, retrieved the birds, and gingerly walked back to their boat, all the way, on top of the water.

He asked his brother what he thought of the dog and the brother replied, *"So, you bought a dog who can't swim."*

How often do the littlest differences or objections begin to breed doubt and disbelief in our lives? Are we confidant in whom we are or do we battle with discouragement, self-confidence and doubt? If we are to be honest with ourselves, every one of us has struggled with doubt at one time or another; doubt over whether we can accomplish a task before us; doubt about whether we could really be loved by another; doubt as to our worth; doubt as to whether Jesus can really save us; doubt as to whether He's coming back; doubt as to whether we truly belong to Him. In each of these instances, Satan attempts to persuade us that we are beyond His love, His forgiveness and His redemption. The enemy works night and day to cast doubt upon the very experience of Christ's death and resurrection. For he knows should he be able to cast a cloud upon our confidence in Christ, that he will stifle our growth and impede our work for the gospel.

As one recalls the story of Thomas and Jesus' appearing to him after His crucifixion, burial and resurrection, we see why Thomas has been dubbed 'Doubting Thomas'; due to his inability to believe something he could not see. Even though Thomas had lived and communed with Christ for 3 years prior to these circumstances; even though Thomas had heard Jesus teach of what must come to pass; even though Thomas had seen Jesus raise others from the dead; the whole idea that Jesus was alive again was beyond what Thomas could accept.

Doubt is a powerful emotion; something that can cripple and paralyze one. In all of the excitement of Christ's resurrection that His disciples and followers were experiencing, Thomas was being plagued by fears, anxiety and doubt. How could this happen? What will we do next? I've spent the last 3 years of my life with Him and now what? Could He really be alive again? How could this be? So many questions; all inspired by what he could not understand. So much that Thomas would declare his disbelief until or unless he was able to actually see for himself. And because of these doubts, Thomas lived in angst and was missing out on so many blessings.

While it is easy for us to cast stones at Thomas to question how he could have ever doubted after all he had seen, have we not seen more and yet still doubt. We have seen thousands of years of prophecy play out before our very eyes and yet we still wonder, we still contemplate and we still doubt. Can God really be taken at His word? Can He really do all that He said? Did He really do what I've read about and been taught? What if it's all been made up? What if it really never happened? These are the doubts and concerns that many deal with every day.

At this point Jesus could have reprimanded Thomas for his doubt but in Christ's loving manner, He simply desired for Thomas to believe. Therefore, Jesus responded, *"Put your finger here, and look at my hands. Put your hand into the wound in my side. Don't be faithless any longer. Believe!"* - John 20:27. All Jesus desires of any of us is that we believe.

Satan has used doubt since the very beginning of time to steer our beliefs and influence our relationship. From as early as the Garden, Satan has attempted to besmirch God's name and cast doubt as to whether God truly meant what He said. All the way at the beginning of the Bible in Genesis 3:1 we see the serpent attempting to muddy the waters as he would ask Eve, *"Did God really say you must not eat the fruit from any of the trees in the garden?"* The art of creating doubt has been one of the enemy's most handily used weapons in the spiritual contest we find ourselves.

Since we thus understand that doubt comes from the very pit of hell, how must we arm ourselves to do battle and prevent the skepticism and apprehension from entering our lives? First, we must realize that we are in a battle and that the enemy, notwithstanding God's strength, is more than we can handle. Therefore, we must as the Psalmist said, *"rise early, before the sun is up; I cry out for help and put my hope in your words"* - Psalm 119:147. Secondly, we need to *"Do not get involved in foolish discussions..."* as described in Titus 3:9. There is an old cliché that says, *"God said it. I believe it. That settles it."* However, regardless of whether we believe it, if God said it, that settles it. Finally, we need to *"I recall all you have done, O Lord;"* - Psalm 77:11. As we reflect on all that God has done for us and as we reflect on all the words He has fulfilled, we should find solace in His words, apart from the doubts of this world.

The encounter of Jesus and Thomas was many years ago and

yet Jesus' words still ring true today. Yes, it is difficult to avoid all doubt; and yes, it is difficult to always believe without being able to see. However, as Smith Wigglesworth once noted, *"I am not moved by what I see. I am not moved by what I feel. I am moved only by what I believe."* As we strive to cast doubt aside and trust in Christ may we claim this promise from our Savior, *"You believe because you have seen me. Blessed are those who believe without seeing me."* While we may never be able to overcome all doubt, let not our lives be characterized as *"Doubting (insert name)"* but as *"Believing (insert name)"*.

Food for Thought

Am I blind in my faith or are my eyes focused on Christ?

_____

_____

_____

_____

_____

Do I believe because Christ said so or do I, as Thomas, have to see? Be specific.

_____

_____

_____

_____

_____

Do I know what I believe and why according to scripture or am I easily persuaded by the whims of another? Explain.

_____

_____

_____

_____

_____

If I truly believe Christ is God, who have I told today?

_____

_____

_____

_____

How can I take God at His word today and begin living with a deep, emboldened faith?

_____

_____

_____

_____

_____

Week 42
IRS
(INNATE REPREHENSIBLE SIN)

We are all infected and impure with sin. When we display our righteous deeds, they are nothing but filthy rags. Like autumn leaves, we wither and fall, and our sins sweep us away like the wind.
- Isaiah 64:6

As many others I'm sure, I heard of a man who purchased a white mouse to use as food for his pet snake. He would drop the unsuspecting mouse into the snake's glass cage, where the snake was sleeping in a bed of sawdust. The tiny mouse had a real predicament on his hands. At any moment he could be swallowed alive. Obviously, the mouse needed to immediately devise a brilliant plan.

How would the terrified creature overcome its dilemma? He quickly went to work covering the snake with sawdust chips until it was completely buried. With that, the mouse apparently thought he had solved his problem.

The solution, however, came from outside. The man took pity on the silly little mouse that he had dropped in and instead removed him from the cage. The lesson to be learned - no matter how hard we try to cover or deny our sinful nature, we are lost on our own and headed toward death and destruction.

That leads us to discuss the most destructive force in all of human history - SIN. From the demise and undoing of Adam and Eve in the Garden of Eden and moving forward, sin has caused pain, misery, heartache, guilt and so much more. Sin has caused one brother to kill another. Sin has caused one man to take another's wife in adultery. Sin has caused the exaltation of man, thereby driving man to worship everything except God Himself. Sin causes a child to lie to his parents, an adult to cheat on his taxes, and a politician to use his office to advance his own interests. Sin causes wars, famines and pestilence. Everything that has ever caused tragedy is rooted in sin; ultimately leading one to physical death and eternal death if not rectified. And regardless how one attempts to overcome his sin nature, apart from God's 'intrusive' healing and forgiveness, he will die in his sin.

God's word is clear regarding the origin of sin, the consequences of sin and the only remedy for sin. While the origin of sin in mankind can be traced to Adam and Eve, sin itself – disobedience to God's laws – was first evidenced in Heaven by Lucifer who would espouse, 'I will ascend to heaven and set my throne above God's stars. I will preside on the mountain of the gods far away in the north. I will climb to the highest heavens and be like the Most High' (Isaiah 14:13-14). Because of the sin of pride, Lucifer was reduced from his prestigious position among God's angels and cast from heaven. As he would take up residence on earth, he made it his continual goal to tempt and lead mankind into sin, rebellion against God and ultimately to subject man to imprisonment under his dictatorship. While sin may appear desirable for a time, it always bears a price. It has been said of sin that it will *"take you farther than you want to go, keep you longer than you want to stay and cost you more than you want to pay."* Additionally, it has been noted, *"Sin wouldn't be so attractive if the wages were paid immediately"*.

So what is the cost for sinning? Well Romans 6:23 tells us, *"The wages **(price to be paid)** of sin is death."* This my friends is not only a physical death but also a spiritual one. For in Romans 2:6-8 we read, *"He will judge everyone according to what they have done. He will give eternal life to those who keep on doing good, seeking after the glory and honor and immortality that God offers. But he will pour out his anger and wrath on those who live for themselves, who refuse to obey the truth and instead live lives of wickedness."* In fact, the Bible talks about the eternal residence those who choose to turn their backs on God will endure in Matthew 25:41 where Jesus said, *"Then the King will turn to those on the left and say, 'Away with you, you cursed ones, into the eternal fire prepared for the devil and his demons'"* Christ would go on to say just a few verses later, *"And these will go away into eternal punishment..."* (vs. 46).

The reality of Hell is not vocalized often enough or loud enough – for if we really grasped the horridness of hell and were burdened for those who are destined to spend eternity apart from God without His intervention, I believe it would drive us to be never-ending in our testimony and proclamation of the gospel. In fact, we read in Matthew 13:42 that there will be *"weeping and gnashing of teeth"*. Also, hell is described as *"everlasting destruction"*, *"eternal punishment"*, a *"blazing furnace where the fire never ceases"*, and where those will be *"put in chains of darkness"*. Hell is as real as heaven; and as beautiful as heaven is, hell is the complete opposite.

Many say, *"How could a loving God possibly send anyone to a place like that?"* Well truth be told, God doesn't send anyone to hell; that is a personal decision made by all. In fact, God intervened out of His grace, mercy and love so as to save all those who would trust in Him from a devil's hell. In all actuality, Hell was originally designed for Satan and his demons (Jude 1:6/II Pet. 2:4) but because of man's sin, he has condemned himself to this same place unless he accepts God's perfect sacrifice in Christ. To this extent, the Bible tells us in Galatians 4:4-5, *"But when the right time came, God sent his Son, born of a woman, subject to the law. God sent him to buy freedom for us who were slaves to the law, so that he could adopt us as his very own children."* Even more, we're told in Romans 5:8, *"But God showed his great love for us by sending Christ to die for us while we were still sinners."* God has done everything He can through the sacrifice of His Son, Jesus Christ, to offer forgiveness, redemption and a future in Heaven rather than Hell. The ball is now in our court.

At the end of the day; at the end of life; it will not be the individual sins of one that will condemn him to Hell – it will be the sin of rejecting Christ, ultimately selfish pride. Sin is innate (inborn) and reprehensible (deplorable). Sin has broken the relationship between God and man; but because of God's great love, *"But God is so rich in mercy, and he loved us so much, that even though we were dead because of our sins, he gave us life when he raised Christ from the dead. (It is only by God's grace that you have been saved!)"* - Eph. 2:4-5, He has created the door we must all enter through. Will we therefore choose to enter through 'the door', His Son, or will we choose to attempt to enter on our own? The 'prizes' behind each door are extremely different – choose correctly.

Food for Thought

What area of sin in my life is as the snake awaiting to devour me?

_____

_____

_____

_____

_____

_____

_____

_____

Sin doesn't bury all at once. In fact, it's generally a slow boil to death. Am I 'playing' with sin today?

_____

_____

_____

_____

_____

Do I really believe sin condemns one to hell? If so, what am I doing to prevent others from attending?

_____

_____

_____

_____

_____

Society has become so immune to the effects of sin today that it isn't even recognized. Am I calling out sin or do I just turn my head?

_____

_____

_____

_____

_____

God promises that He will, *"lay the sins of the parents upon their children; the entire family is affected—even children in the third and fourth generations of those who reject me."* - Ex. 20:5. Am I protecting or endangering my children and grandchildren? Explain.

_____

_____

_____

_____

_____

_____

_____

_____

✝

Week 43
NO REAR VIEW
VISION

God answered, "I will be with you. And this is your sign that I am the one who has sent you: When you have brought the people out of Egypt, you will worship God at this very mountain."
- Exodus 3:12

History records how on May 6, 1954, Roger Bannister became the first man ever to run a mile in less than 4 minutes. Within 2 months, John Landy eclipsed the record by 1.4 seconds. However, on August 7, 1954, the two met together for a historic race. As they moved into the last lap, Landy held the lead. Bannister was nowhere to be seen and it looked as if Landy would win, but as he neared the finish he was haunted by the question, *"Where is Bannister?"* As he turned to look over his shoulder, Bannister took the lead. Landy later told a Time magazine reporter, *"If I hadn't looked back, I would have won!"*

How many times in life do we find ourselves as John Landy ...looking back? Whether it be in athletics or life, the act of looking back minimizes the value of the present and the hope for the future. Many throughout the Bible have looked backed to an earlier time thinking, *"Oh how I wish I could still be there."* Take for instance the children of Israel in the wilderness. In Exodus 16:3 we read, *"If only the Lord had killed us back in Egypt,"* they moaned. *"There we sat around pots filled with meat and ate all the bread we wanted. But now you have brought us into this wilderness to starve us all to death."* Then there was Lot's wife, when fleeing the destruction that would befall Sodom, *"looked back and turned into a pillar of salt."* Our vision needs to be forever focused on what lies ahead, not what lies behind remembering as C.S. Lewis noted, *"There are far, far better things ahead than any we leave behind."*

The act of looking back simply glorifies ancient history – and while appearing to have an alluring nature, the past acts as an obstacle to the great feats within our grasp. Thinking back to the illustration of Bannister and Landy, the moment Landy looked back was the moment he lost the race. While this physical test of endurance would have been nice to win, how many lose out on blessings in life and possibly fail to lay hold on eternal life because of looking back? Indeed, the Christian life is designed to be constantly forward looking, pushing forward and *"pressing on to reach the end of the race and receive the heavenly prize for which God, through Christ Jesus, is calling us"* - Philippians 3:14. So, what are the obstacles that cause us to look back, losing step and possibly the race?

As we are all too familiar with, this life we live is filled with hectic busy times mixed with colorful temptations. In addition, as human beings we have a knack for focusing on the good times that may have been splintered between bad times but we also somehow seem to make past experiences seem grander than they truly were. These tactics are simply spiritual military strategies employed by the enemy to take our eyes off of Christ and the finish line; in so, causing many a victorious Christian to simply become another defeated combatant.

There is no wonder why the Bible paints the picture so often of the Christian life as an athletic event. From the description of remaining focused on the finish line to the fact that only one wins in a race to the crowds of spectators that sit watching in the stands of life, the way we live out our Christian life matters not only to us but to those around us. With this in mind, we need to be forever vigilant to the potential obstacles that lie in wait looking to trip us and cause us to fall.

In races and in life the only one that is remembered is the one who wins; the rest become faded images within a thousand names. At the same time, it does not mean that victory will come without adversity. The key to success in the Christian life is to stop looking back, to get up when one falls, and to keep our eyes firmly affixed on Jesus Christ. A sports story is told how during a Monday night football game featuring the Chicago Bears and the New York Giants, one of the announcers noted how Walter Payton had accumulated over nine miles in career rushing yards. The other announcer responded, *"Yeah, and that's with someone knocking him down every 4.6 yards!"* Walter Payton understood that everyone --even the very best-- get knocked down. The key to success is to get up and run again just as hard. Walter Payton demonstrated what one can accomplish when they do not look back, content with what they have accomplished, but continue to see the goal line in front of them every time they are handed the ball.

May we always approach our Christian life as Henry Wadsworth Longfellow described, *"Look not mournfully into the past, it comes not back again. Wisely improve the present, it is thine. Go forth to meet the shadowy future without fear and with a manly heart."* Winners never look back for they know the prize is in front of them.

Food for Thought

Is my past consistently drawing me back?

_____

_____

_____

_____

_____

How can I be successful if I'm constantly looking back?

_____

_____

_____

_____

_____

The old expression says, *"If the grass is greener, it's generally because there's more manure to shovel"*. Why do I long for the manure of yesterday instead of the milk and honey of tomorrow?

_____

_____

_____

_____

_____

Does my future reflect heaven or hell? If heaven, why am I still bogged down in the mire of this world?

_____

_____

_____

_____

Another expression says, *"If the devil reminds you of your past, remind him of his future."* The only way to combat the past is to delve into the Word. Am I spending time daily in the Word? Truly evaluate.

_____

_____

_____

_____

_____

✝

Week 44
300

The Lord told Gideon, "With these 300 men I will rescue you and give you victory over the Midianites. Send all the others home."
- Judges 7:7

The Battle of Thermopylae (480 BC) is a historical event that has ballooned into a theatrical extravaganza in the movie, simply named, 300. The story tells of the battle waged between an alliance of Greek city-states, led by King Leonidas of Sparta, and the Persian Empire led by Xerxes, over the course of three days during the second Persian invasion of Greece. After days of warring, non-stop action, the Persians managed to obtain the upper hand with the help of a traitor, Ephiates, who would reveal information to Xerxes that would provide for a total ambush and annihilation of thousands, leaving simply 300 Spartans to defend and hold the line as most of the Greek army would be dismissed and ordered to retreat. The philosophy of Tacitus who remarked, *"He that fights and runs away, may turn and fight another day; But he that is in battle slain, will never rise to fight again"* would be on full display that day. Unfortunately, for the 300 Spartans and many other Greeks, the Persian Empire would amass an enormous victory, where thousands would lay dead and Athens laid waste, at the end of the melee. On this day, though many valiant warriors would shed their blood and give their lives, demonstrating that 300 men was simply not enough to fend off an estimated 100,000-150,000 Persian warriors.

This however was not the first battle in history where an army of 300 soldiers would tackle that of an estimated 135,000 trained military personnel. In fact, almost 800 years previous, Gideon would lead a small band of men against the Midianites. After Gideon's commissioning by God to lead an army against the wicked Midianite regime, and Gideon's continual push back, Gideon finally accepted that God had a plan in mind to bring freedom once again to His people.

At this time Gideon would begin to recruit and construct an army to oppose the Midianites; however, even after his attempts at recruiting, he was only able assemble an army of 32,000 – to oppose 135,000. As if the odds were not bad enough, God instructed Gideon that his force was too large. *"Too large? It was already a 4 to 1 ratio of soldiers. How could this company be too large?"* Nevertheless, Gideon listened to and obeyed God.

In order for the first cuts to take place, Gideon instructed the people saying, *"Whoever is timid or afraid may leave this mountain and go home."* - Judges 7:3. Once those who were not cut out for battle thinned the lines, Gideon was now left with a remaining 10,000 men. While the battle had gone from a shaky 4:1 ratio, it was now at a precarious 13.5:1 ratio. And as nervous and uncertain as Gideon was initially, he must have been beside himself at this point. However, again God spoke to Gideon telling him, *"The people are still too many...."* *"What in the world are you talking about God?"* Gideon must have thought. *"While I realize these may be the best and bravest that Israel has to offer, how are we going to win against such unrealistic odds?"* These and many other questions, I'm sure, raced through Gideon's mind, yet at the same time, Gideon obeyed.

Gideon now took the men down to a local brook and was given instructions by God as to what to look for in the remaining bunch. *"Divide the men into two groups. In one group put all those who cup water in their hands and lap it up with their tongues like dogs. In the other group put all those who kneel down and drink with their mouths in the stream."* - Judges 7:5. Then the Lord said to Gideon, *"With these 300 men I will rescue you and give you victory over the Midianites. Send all the others home."* - Judges 7:7. WHAT?! You got to be kidding me! 300 men against 135,000?! That's a 450:1 ratio!

Let's be honest, every one of us would have been thinking the same thing. While we say to ourselves, *"I trust you God, in the back of our minds, we're like – really?"* Faith is believing and acting on what we cannot prove, and this is where Gideon found himself. No one would have blamed Gideon for doubting how a simple band of 300 men would be able to destroy an elite and massive fighting force. Yet, Gideon trusted God to bring the victory.

At this time, Gideon began to devise military strategies with his top advisors as to how they would tackle this 'giant'. But before long, God spoke to Gideon again in a dream describing how the battle was already his for the taking. So Gideon proceeded to tell the men, *"Get up! For the Lord has given you victory over the Midianite hordes!"* - Judges 7:15. Then he divided the three hundred men into three companies, and he put a trumpet into every man's hand, with empty pitchers, and torches inside the pitchers. And he said to them, *"Then he said to them, "Keep your eyes on me. When I come to the edge of the camp, do just as I do. 18 As soon as I and those with me blow the rams' horns, blow your horns, too, all around the entire camp, and shout, 'For the Lord and for Gideon!'"* - Judges 7:17-18.

When all the men were in position, Gideon initiated the attack. It was at this time that the Midianites, thinking they were being ambushed by thousands, began to wield their swords, thus killing each other by the thousands. That day the Lord handed the army of the Midianites into the hands of the Israelites.

So, you ask, *"What was the difference between the 300 Israelites and the 300 Spartans?"* The answer is simple...GOD. God is the reason for the success of one group and the annihilation of another. God was the One who brought the victory. In fact, from the very beginning of calling Gideon to this task, God told him, *"The Lord said to Gideon, 'You have too many warriors with you. If I let all of you fight the Midianites, the Israelites will boast to me that they saved themselves by their own strength.'"* - Judges 7:2. How often do we find ourselves relying on and boasting about how we made it in life; about how we overcame difficulties; about how we are self-sufficient and in need of help from no one? This is what God knew would be the case with His people.

In order that we may see the hand of God alive and at work in our lives we must face, confront and refute the pride of self. We read in Psalm 118:8, *"It is better to take refuge in the Lord than to trust in people."* Gideon, like Leonidas, could have felt that despite the numbers disadvantage, they were the dominant military force and, would at the strength of their own hands, achieve the victory. Yet instead, Gideon trusted God and was able to experience a 'military victory' that would stand the test of time. May we learn to live what we have seen Gideon exhibit and what Spurgeon cited, *"While others are congratulating themselves, I have to lie humbly at the foot of Christ's cross and marvel that I am saved at all."*

Food for Thought

Am I focused on the numbers around me and against me, or do I believe God is enough?

_____

_____

_____

_____

_____

What are the 'cuts' that God is putting me through to ensure I am a strong soldier for Him?

_____

_____

_____

_____

_____

Just as Gideon faced doubt with the size of the army God was giving him, what doubts am I facing today in my faith walk?

_____

_____

_____

_____

_____

How can I set aside my pride and watch God bring the victory in my life?

_____

_____

_____

_____

_____

Gideon's army needed only lanterns and pitches to experience the victory because God went before them. How can I utilize the 'tools' God has given me to carry forth the victory?

_____

_____

_____

_____

_____

✝

Week 45
TWO HEADED PIRANHA

And so the Lord says, "These people say they are mine. They honor me with their lips, but their hearts are far from me. And their worship of me is nothing but man-made rules learned by rote."
- Isaiah 29:13

The story of Lot and the cities of Sodom and Gomorrah is well-known. The Bible tells us how when Abraham and Lot's people started to bicker and feud, that Abraham allowed Lot first selection as to the area of land that he would dwell while Abraham and his tribe would take the other. Lot, not showing respect for his uncle and desiring only the best for himself, decided to establish residency *"at the fertile plains of the Jordan Valley in the direction of Zoar"*. The Bible describes how *"the whole area was well watered everywhere, like the garden of the LORD"*. - Gen. 13:10. As Lot set up 'camp' in the Jordan Valley, Abraham settled in the land of Canaan. However, as circumstances would have it, Lot was not content to stay on his original homestead. Instead, he *"moved his tents to a place near*

Sodom and settled among the cities of the plain." - Gen. 13:12. The problem with this decision was that the cities of Sodom and Gomorrah were extremely wicked.

Like most people who fall into a backslidden position with God, Lot continued to become more engrossed in the culture and sin of the land. In fact, within a short time Lot moved into the city itself – everyday becoming more accepting of the gross sin of the land and less effective in the lives of his family. While Lot continued to know what was morally right, as his uncle Abraham had taught him, he chose to neglect the importance of God's standards. So much, that when he eventually became an official at the gate of the city, he found himself having no influence.

However, the double-mindedness and the lack of influence didn't stop there. As God's word shows, when angels were sent to forewarn him of the impending judgment of God, that only Lot, his wife and their two young daughters were able to escape the city before its destruction. Lot lost his other two daughters and sons-in-law because he refused to stand for right and instead chose to accept sin and its consequences. Even more, Lot lost his wife, who would turn her head in disobedience to God, thus costing her life. Lot had lost all that really mattered in life – his faith, his family and his testimony- because of his pursuit for possessions and position. Ultimately, we see the effects of a man who is unstable, unfixed in his faith and ambivalent in all his convictions.

The Bible has much to say about fickle and capricious behaviors of men and, better yet, has painted the picture for us in so many different examples. In fact, Christians are warned and encouraged in James 4:8, *"Come close to God, and God will come close to you. Wash your hands, you sinners; purify your hearts, for your loyalty is divided between God and the world."* While as a people, we see the example of Israel and the correlation to America which can be made in Hosea 10:1-2, *"How prosperous Israel is — a luxuriant vine loaded with fruit. But the richer the people get, the more pagan altars they build. The more bountiful their harvests, the more beautiful their sacred pillars."* There is no argument that America is an extremely wealthy nation; yet in amassing such wealth the Church has become like Lot, living in sin and ineffective, 'at the gates' of societal influence. D.L. Moody described it as, *"We can stand affliction better than we can prosperity, for in prosperity we forget God."*

The sin of double-mindedness is a slow, cancerous sin that infects, hijacks and metastasizes in the life of an individual. It is a sin that causes one to slowly but progressively accept and condone sin from one level to another. And it is a sin that causes a complete disintegration of all that one knows and holds to be true. Lot experienced this sin in multiple fold as he began to doubt and flex between what God had taught him through Abraham and what he allowed the world to plant within his mind and soul. Unlike the sins of murder and adultery which many would outright condemn as wrong and evil, the sin of insipidness often remains cloaked and beneath the surface, often being rationalized as the growth of one to alter their beliefs based upon information rather than knowledge.

Many an individual has had an experience with a person he considered a 'friend' only to witness the act of two-facedness. This may have been through kind words spoken to his face only to learn of wrong and hurtful words spoken behind his back or it could have possibly been one who found his company to be acceptable while he had something to offer only until a 'better offer' came along. Regardless, anyone who has endured such conduct has most certainly felt betrayed and hurt through such actions. This my friends is the epitome of the term double-minded. It is the behavior of one who 'speaks out both sides of his mouth'. This person cannot be trusted.

Hence, the act of double-mindedness is actually an inaction to stand for what one believes to be right. Instead this individual allows the tides of the day or the opinions of another to sway him. This man is wholly and completely without conviction and cannot be counted upon when the times get tough. He dares not rock the boat for fear of falling over. Double-mindedness, in a man, perpetuates the belief in a believer that he can be a Christian and still be part of a fallen society. It causes him to question whether God is correct or really 'meant it'. And it prevents him from being seen differently, thus removing his godly testimony and influence on others. All such people would be wise to reflect upon James 4:4, *"You adulterers! Don't you realize that friendship with the world makes you an enemy of God? I say it again: If you want to be a friend of the world, you make yourself an enemy of God."*

Wavering in one's faith, knowledge and relationship with Christ creates a stumbling block for the sinner in need of a

Savior looking to us as the reflection of a loving God. In fact, Oswald Chambers once wrote, *"If in preaching the gospel you substitute your knowledge of the way of salvation for confidence in the power of the gospel, you hinder people from getting to reality."*

Christians today need to stop floundering in the Word of God; believers need to become rooted in the Word and to proclaim it loudly and proudly; and Christ-followers need to exhibit a spiritual intestinal fortitude. God never commands us to do something or to forsake something without letting us know why – our role is to study and understand the implications. Thus a man who is double-minded, two-faced, faithless, erratic in behavior or insipid is not a man, but a babe that is ungrounded in his faith and the Word of God. Today is the day we begin growing up and living as Luther encouraged, *"People must have righteous principals in the first, and then they will not fail to perform virtuous actions."*

Food for Thought

Am I being pulled away from God in my faith walk? If so, what can I do to get back on track? If not, it's time to get to work.

_____

_____

_____

_____

_____

Does my 'yea' mean 'yea' or am I tossed between in my beliefs dependent upon the circles I travel? Explain.

_____

_____

_____

_____

_____

Is my life distinctly different from those of the world? Be specific.

_____

_____

_____

_____

_____

Am I trying to live the Christian life with one foot still in the world? Have I 'sold-out' for the cause of the cross? What does scripture say about protecting our witness and be part of the world?

_____

_____

_____

_____

How can I share the gospel with those in 'Sodom' this week?

_____

_____

_____

_____

_____

_____

_____

✝

Week 46
PRICELESS

I knew you before I formed you in your mother's womb. Before you were born I set you apart...
- Jeremiah 1:5

There are some things money can't buy – love, happiness, and eternal security. MasterCard believes they can fill this void. So much, that they have created a very famous and catchy slogan. While many people chase money and while money can buy (or at least rent) many things, there are some things that are more valuable than money: for instance – YOU!

I'm sure that everyone reading this has at one time wished they could be more like someone else or even wished they could be someone else. Life in pictures always looks better than in person but it's hard not to think we could be so much more or that we have fallen short of dreams and goals. How great would it be to...? How much better would my life be if...? Why I can't be...? These, and others, are the secret questions that rob our joy and deprive the world of our uniqueness.

Satan often tries to attack us through making us feel insufficient, inferior or inadequate but God believes we are made perfect in His image. In fact, if you were not such a precious and unique individual why would God have had to give His life for you? Think about it, while John 3:16 tells us, *"For this is how God loved the world:"*, if the world had simply and solely consisted of you, Jesus would still have died for YOU!

In Real Estate the key to the difference in all properties, and therefore pricing, is known as uniqueness; all property is different yet special. Why would anyone want to live in a cookie-cutter mold of a home when they could own and live in a home that was different than all those around? While people look for distinctive characteristics in homes and a sense of individualism, why is it that they don't value and appreciate the significance of their own individuality?

While it has become a cliché to *"Be the best YOU you can be because there's only one you"*, the truth is not minimized. When we try to be someone else or just aren't happy with who we are, we devalue ourselves and rob the world of what we have to offer. What would the world be like if everyone was a top race car driver yet there was not a mechanic to ensure the speed and safety of the car? Or what if everyone was a doctor but there were no nurses to actually care for the patients? Or what if everyone desired to be a principal or textbook author but there were no teachers to lay the foundation for our children? Everyone is special; everyone is unique; and everyone is necessary for the full functioning of our society. Here is a great example to demonstrate the importance and value of who you are and what you have to share.

An old Chinese proverb describes the value of understanding and appreciating one's unique abilities. It says, *"There was once a stone cutter who was dissatisfied with himself and with his position in life.*

One day he passed a wealthy merchant's house. Through the open gateway, he saw many fine possessions and important visitors. 'How powerful that merchant must be!' thought the stone cutter. He became very envious and wished that he could be like the merchant.

To his great surprise, he suddenly became the merchant, enjoying more luxuries and power than he had ever imagined, but was envied and detested by those less wealthy than himself. Soon a high official passed by, carried in a sedan chair, accompanied by attendants and escorted by soldiers beating gongs. Everyone, no matter how wealthy, had to bow low before the procession. 'How powerful that official is!' he thought. 'I wish that I could be a high official!'

Then he became the high official, carried everywhere in his embroidered sedan chair, feared and hated by the people all around. It was a hot summer day, so the official felt very uncomfortable in the sticky sedan chair. He looked up at the sun. It shone proudly in the sky, unaffected by his presence. 'How powerful the sun is!" he thought. "I wish that I could be the sun!'

Then he became the sun, shining fiercely down on everyone, scorching the fields, cursed by the farmers and laborers. But a huge black cloud moved between him and the earth, so that his light could no longer shine on everything below. 'How powerful that storm cloud is!' he thought. 'I wish that I could be a storm cloud!'

Then he became the storm cloud, flooding the fields and villages, shouted at by everyone. But soon he found that he was being pushed away by some great force, and realized that it was the wind. 'How powerful it is!' he thought. 'I wish that I could be the wind!'

Then he became the wind, blowing tiles off the roofs of houses, uprooting trees, feared and hated by all below him. But after a while, he ran up against something that would not move, no matter how forcefully he blew against it – a huge, towering rock. 'How powerful that rock is!' he thought. 'I wish that I could be a rock!'

Then he became the rock, more powerful than anything else on earth. But as he stood there, he heard the sound of a hammer pounding a chisel into the hard surface, and felt himself being changed. 'What could be more powerful than I, the rock?' he thought.

He looked down and saw far below him the figure of a stone cutter."

Today, stop wishing you were someone else and thank God you are an incalculable jewel in His eyes. Then go out and make a difference in the world He has placed you! There is only one YOU and YOU ARE PRICELESS!

Food for Thought

Do I truly understand my value in Christ? Am I living like it?

_____

_____

_____

_____

_____

Do I treat others as priceless creation of the Holy God of Heaven? How ought I to treat those of like faith and those whom I disagree with?

_____

_____

_____

_____

_____

Dale Carnegie used to say, _"Names are the sweetest and most important sound in any language."_ Do I make it a practice to learn others' names?

_____

_____

_____

_____

_____

Christ not only knows my name but He died for my name. Do I understand the priceless value of such a gift? Am I sharing this gift with others?

_____

_____

_____

_____

_____

Am I thankful for who God made me and how He made me or am I, in essence, telling God He made a mistake? If He made a mistake, why would He have died for a 'mistake'?

_____

_____

_____

_____

_____

✝

Week 47
WHY ME?

But Moses protested to God, "Who am I to
appear before Pharaoh? Who am I to lead
the people of Israel out of Egypt?"
- Exodus 3:11

Imagine if you were, what it would be like to be raised in complete affluence; to have every whim or desire your heart could wish for at your beckoned request. To be trained by the most knowledgeable of teachers, to have others wait on you hand and foot and to never lack for anything. All of this, when in reality, your life should have been snuffed out as a child. Additionally, to have all of this wealth and pleasure at your feet while the rest of your family, friends and countrymen live in slavery and bondage. Then one day you happen to be out walking around and witness complete brutality. Before you consider the ramifications, you pounce into action, breaking the law and jeopardizing your own life. Immediately you know what you've done is beyond forgiveness and you run – you run as far away, as fast as you can before anyone realizes you're gone.

Now living in a foreign land with a fake identity and not knowing who you can trust, you simply wallow through life. Then one day while at work God Himself speaks to you. At first you think you must simply be hearing things; you must be even more tired than you thought or maybe the heat is so horrific that you must be close to fainting. Then there it is again, a small simple voice. You look around, but it's late, and no one else is there. Suddenly, through an unbelievable show of power, God reveals Himself and says, *"I've got a job for you!"* You think to yourself, and whether you actually spoke it or just thought it (who knows because God can hear both), you exclaim, *"Why me? Who am I? Do you know who I am or what I have done?"* And then you remember, of course He does, He's God.

Many might think to themselves, this sure sounds like Moses, and you would be correct – but this is also the story of so many others. All too often we allow the past mistakes of our lives to dictate and direct the future paths and course of our lives. We allow the wrong decisions of old to bind us, imprison us and define us when in fact the past should not restrict us but should serve to prepare us for what God's future in us will unfold.

There is no debate that many find it easier to ignore the prodding of God or to wallow in one's self-pity than to rise to the challenge and answer the call. In fact, the enemy would have us to believe that because of the wrong doings, bad decisions or blatant sins we have committed that God no longer has a use for us. However, he also knows that there is nothing we can do and nothing that we cannot do that will separate us from God or prevent God from using our lives. In fact, Rick Warren once noted, *"If God only used perfect people, nothing would get done. God will use anybody if you're available."*

The Christian life is not about being perfect and God does not choose to use those who seem to have it all together. Quite the opposite, the only requirement that God has in order to use one is that he be available. Throughout the Bible we read story after story of God's intervention in a person's life and how God would take the perceived most wretched and worthless and turn them into shining beacons of His grace and mercy. In fact, I Corinthians 1:27 tells us, *"Instead, God chose things the world considers foolish in order to shame those who think they are wise. And he chose things that are powerless to shame those who are powerful"*. Additionally, we can recall how Paul would say, *"Each time he said, 'My grace is all you need. My power works best in weakness.' So now I am glad to boast about my weaknesses, so that the power of Christ can work through me. That's why I take pleasure in my weaknesses, and in the insults, hardships, persecutions and troubles that I suffer for Christ. For when I am weak, then I am strong"* - II Corinthians 12:9-10.

The question that many choose to ask, *"Why me?"* actually has nothing to do with me but everything to do with Him. God does not need us but He chooses to allow us to partake in His work. At the same time, the time has come for us to stop making excuses or suggesting why God cannot use us. If God could use the likes of Moses - a murderer, David - an adulterer, Paul - a persecutor of believers and so many more, God can use anyone. Even more so, the world needs for us to allow God to work in us and through us. The Marines have a slogan, *"A few good men"*. Well God is looking for a few available men.

When will we begin to realize that we do not need to fit our ideal to be used of God? When will we refuse to oppose God's work in our lives? And when will we begin to cry out as Martin Luther King, Jr. did when he said, *"Use me, God. Show me how to take who I am, who I want to be, and what I can do, and use it for a purpose greater than myself."* It's time to stop asking *"Why Me?"* and begin asking *"Why not Me?"*

Food for Thought

Have I ever thought, *"How can God use me?"* Have I ever thought, *"How can I not let God use me?"* Explain.

_____

_____

_____

_____

_____

Do I allow my past to dictate my future? Be specific.

_____

_____

_____

_____

Do I understand that all God needs is my availability not my ability?

_____

_____

_____

_____

_____

According to scripture, who am I most impressed that God used when I consider his life? Now, if God used him, what have I done that makes me think I'm beyond use?

_____

_____

_____

_____

_____

This week may I begin asking God to use me; then list 1 way in which God can use me.

_____

_____

_____

_____

_____

✝

Week 48
WHEN THE PAST COMES CALLING

But forget all that— it is nothing compared to what I am going to do. For I am about to do something new. See, I have already begun! Do you not see it?
- Isaiah 43:18-19

Years ago it was reported in a local newspaper how Matilda Kaye Crabtree, 14, of West Monroe, LA, used to try to scare her father as a joke. However, one day she made a tragic blunder. She had planned to sleep over at a friend's house but instead stayed home, hid in a closet and then made scary noises as her parents entered the house. Immediately, her father grabbed his .357- caliber pistol. *"Boo!"* she shouted as she jumped out of the closet. Instantly he shot hit her in the neck without realizing it was merely his daughter. Both knowing she would soon be dead, her final words to him were, *"I love you, Daddy."*

Imagine how this father must have felt; not only in the immediate moments after this horrific, accidental tragedy but in the days, weeks, months and years to follow. While the incident was a complete accident, this poor man had lost his daughter, at his own hands, and would now have to live with the images and memories for the remainder of his life.

The past can be a very formidable foe. While not all of us have memories so horrendous, we all do have memories of the past that seem to haunt us. Choices, decisions, actions, words spoken, which seem to relentlessly pursue and hound us. The past can be filled with many wonderful remembrances of yesteryear or the past can be a jail cell that robs us of the present joy and a hopeful future. Unfortunately, when one gets caught up in the confines of their mind, they begin to create a prison of sorts to achieving their full potential and living the life that God has designed and promised.

You see, if he can convince you that for the reason of failed opportunities or actions committed you are unworthy and will never succeed, then he has won; for he has trapped you in a state of fear and angst and has prevented you from moving forward in the power of Christ to enjoy the mountaintops and to endure the valleys.

Haunting memories of action or inaction are often onslaughts by the devil himself. You see, if he can convince you that for the reason of failed opportunities or actions committed you are unworthy and will never succeed, then he has won; for he has trapped you in a state of fear and angst and has prevented you from moving forward in the power of Christ to enjoy the mountaintops and to endure the valleys. The ghosts of the past can be very real; they can be extremely intimidating; and they can be debilitating and paralyzing. And as overwhelming as the ghosts can be, they are no match for the God we serve, who not only redeemed us from our sin but has *"removed our sins as far from us as the east is from the west"* - Ps. 103:12.

As humans we have a propensity to focus on the negative as opposed to the positive; to see the glass half empty instead of half full. This mentality carries over to the way we allow our past to have a greater impact on our lives than we do in relishing the present and looking forward to the future with hope and cheer. Helen Keller, one who had so much that she could have let drag her down, once commented, *"Be of good cheer. Do not think of today's failures, but of the success that may come tomorrow. You have set yourselves a difficult task, but you will succeed if you persevere; and you will find a joy in overcoming obstacles. Remember, no effort that we make to attain something beautiful is ever lost."*

God has not only told us to forget about yesterday; inclusive of the sins, the short-comings, the broken promises, the missed opportunities and the lost time. He has also exhorted us to live in the present, to look forward to the bright and beautiful future He has prepared for us and to not miss any of it along the way. As cliché as it has become it is still a truth that will stand all time, when Satan reminds you of your past, remind him of his future.

Don't allow yourself to live in the mistakes of yesterday which rob you of today's joys. Yesterday can never be changed and tomorrow has yet to be written. Enjoy Today!

Food for Thought

Am I being plagued by my past? If so, what memory is it that is the enemy is using?

_____

_____

_____

_____

_____

_____

How can I use my past as an example to others that God can forgive and use instead of condemning and haunting?

_____

_____

_____

_____

_____

_____

Realizing that the past can never be changed, why do I choose to dwell there instead of in the present and looking forward to the future?

_____

_____

_____

_____

The Bible tells us in II Corinthians 5:17, *"This means that anyone who belongs to Christ has become a new person. The old life is gone; a new life has begun!"* How can I claim and apply this promise as I 'let go and let God'?

_____

_____

_____

_____

Today, when Satan reminds me of my past, let me remind him of his future.

Week 49
UNANSWERED
PRAYERS

*And even when you ask, you don't get it
because your motives are all wrong—you
want only what will give you pleasure.*
- James 4:3

In 1990 Garth Brooks produced his album, No Fences, which contained the extremely popular hit, Unanswered Prayers. While the theology isn't necessarily the best, the sentiment plays exactly along the way that many believers feel all too often in their prayer life. The storyline refers to a man that runs into a high school sweetheart at a football game, one Friday night while out with his wife. Looking back on the way he felt and the desire he had to spend his life with this girl, only to find out his prayers weren't answered, he comes to the realization that it wasn't that his prayers weren't answered, they just weren't answered the way he thought they should be or in his timeframe.

As a people we seem to think that God should answer our

prayers immediately and word for word the way we petitioned for them. It could be because we live in such a time where folks are used to getting immediate satisfaction; it could be because we believe we know what's best; or it could be because we simply treat God as our magical genie, only there to grant every request we have. The greater shame is that when or if we don't receive an answer immediately we begin to believe God doesn't care. In all actuality, God may be testing us to see how much we long for our request or if it's just a fleeting whim. Or God may just be teaching us, stretching our faith and storing up for us a much greater blessing than we can imagine. At the same time God may not be answering our prayer because of disobedience in our own life. In fact, the Psalmist tells us in Psalm 66:18, *"If I had not confessed the sin in my heart, the Lord would not have listened."*

Prayer is not simply an act of making requests based upon a laundry list; it is not designed to deliver us our every want on our timeline; and the basis of whether it has been answered or not should not be judged on immediate evidence or circumstances. Indeed, to truly receive from God His best, our prayer should have the intent of experiencing His will being accomplished in our lives.

Regarding how God decides to answer prayer, a story is told about His unconventional means. It appears while Josh McDowell was a seminary student in California his father passed and went home to Heaven. Josh's mother had died a number of years previous but he was never sure if she knew Christ as her personal Savior. This led Josh to become very depressed, wondering if she might have been lost. Was she a Christian or not? This was the persisting question that haunted him. *"Lord,"* he prayed, *"somehow give me the answer so I can get back to normal. I've just got to know."* It seemed like an unimaginable plea.

Two days later as Josh was driving out to the ocean, he parked and walked to the end of a pier for some alone time. Unbeknownst to him was an old woman sitting in a lawn chair fishing. This is how God would soon answer Josh's prayer and provide the unsearchable answer from beyond the gates of Heaven. *"Where you from son?"* she asked.

"Michigan -- Union City," Josh replied. *"Nobody's heard of it. I tell people it's a suburb of --"* *"Battle Creek,"* interrupted the woman. *"Yeah, I had a cousin from there. Did you happen to know the McDowell family?"*

Astonished, Josh replied, *"Yes ma'am. I'm Josh McDowell!"*

"Amazing!" said the woman. *"Your mother was my cousin."*

"Do you remember anything about her spiritual life?" Josh inquired. *"I sure do – when your mom and I were teenagers we attended a tent revival in town. I believe it was the fourth night when we both went forward to accept Christ as Savior."*

"Thank you Jesus!" Josh roared, alarming the nearby fishermen.

God may not always answer prayer on our timeline but never

doubt that He will answer. Saints of God, take heart, our God answers prayer...ALWAYS! However, sometimes the problem isn't that God doesn't care but it's that we just aren't listening.

Food for Thought

How strong is my prayer life today? Is it a 'wish list' or a time of worship?

_____

_____

_____

_____

_____

The Bible says in Psalm 66:18, *"If I don't confess the sin in my heart, the Lord would not listen."* In the moments that God seems silent toward my prayer, do I take the time to ensure my relationship is pure with Him?

_____

_____

_____

_____

_____

How 'aggressively' do I pursue Christ's working in my life through prayer? (Read Matt. 7:7-12)

_____

_____

_____

_____

_____

If I desire to be in God's will, do I accept when He says 'No' as well as when He says 'Yes'?

_____

_____

_____

_____

_____

Am I so in tune with God that I see the answers to my prayers in ways that may seem subtle? Explain.

_____

_____

_____

_____

_____

_____

_____

_____

✝

Week 50
TURNING LIONS
INTO KITTENS

Daniel answered, "Long live the king! My
God sent his angel to shut the lions' mouths
so that they would not hurt me"...
- Daniel 6:21-22

Many of us can recall the story of Daniel and the lions' den from our years as a child in Sunday school class. Unfortunately for many it's simply just that...a nice story. However, for Daniel it was as real as it can get and there are many lessons we can learn from this amazing feat of protection Daniel experienced.

For many of us we look forward to our golden years with regard to a prospective retirement but not for Daniel. If we are blessed enough to make it into our eighties, we certainly don't expect to be working, let alone ruling. And the thought that our faith and the consequential actions could land us in prison, or worse an execution, are generally the furthest from our minds. Whether we are in our twenties or our eighties, do we believe that God can use us and save us from the treacherous actions of others?

Daniel had been employed in the service of many kings at this point for roughly sixty years. He had demonstrated integrity, faith and conviction in many different settings. God had used him to share remarkable lessons about the future, about impending punishment, about the rise of one nation at the expense of another; and through it all God had never forsaken Daniel. God had taken a young boy and molded him into a servant of the Most High, placing him on the main stage of history. Forever Daniel will be remembered as a courageous, faithful leader who trusted God but was Daniel any different than you or me? Is it possible that we can become a present day Daniel? When faced with opposition and possible persecution how do we choose to respond? Do we complain and question God or do we thank Him for working in our lives to strengthen and develop us?

Daniel had become a very trusted and revered advisor, politician and, even friend, of the current ruler, Darius. However, in so doing, Daniel had also developed enemies; those who wanted nothing more than to see the death of this man of God simply because he would not conform to their ways. And they would stop at nothing to ensure Daniel was removed from the equation.

As we read the story in Daniel 6, Daniel's adversaries had become weary of Darius comparing them to Daniel and thus highlighting Daniel's superior performance. They sought their own agenda and simply would not allow this 'Jew' to stand in their way. While they sought for a reason, turning over every rock and even constructing some of their own, they could find nothing to damage Daniel's reputation. Their rage and jealousy continued to mount and they knew if they were to further their selfish ambitions then they would need to take their game to the next level.

So it was decided they would concoct a plan that would prey on and feed off of the insecurities and arrogance of a pagan ruler who actually believed he could be a deity. They proposed that the king establish a 30-day law that prohibited everyone from praying to or worshipping anyone other than the king himself. The price for breaking such a law would mean the culprit would become the main course for a den of hungry lions.

While the consequence must have been terrifying, I mean, imagine being ripped apart at the hands of lions! Despite the very real possibility, neither the actions of such adversaries or the royal law would discourage Daniel from participating in his daily practice of communing with God in prayer. Not only did Daniel continue to pray to God but he would pray three times a day and he by no means tried to hide it. Daniel would retire to his house, open his doors and windows and bow before his God in humble adoration. It was for this reason that Daniel would be thrown to the lions in what one would expect to be the end. But what we know about God is that what may seem like the end to man is just the beginning for God.

Upon further reading we know that Daniel was thrown to the lions, the den was sealed and the king was left regretting his decision; but we also know how through this God would not only deliver His man but would show Himself as the only true God to a pagan king. It's amazing how God continues to seek out and draw so many to Himself!

When morning arrived Darius raced to the den anticipating and imploring Daniel's response from beyond the seal. As Daniel was retrieved from the den, it was witnessed how not a scratch lay upon his body or clothes. There was no other proof needed to transform an unbeliever into a believing man. As I'm sure Daniel would have responded, *"My king, My God and King has saved me. While I've never seen such hungry lions before, my God made them like kittens. He sent His angel to protect me and those lions they cowered in the corner all night. I've never seen anything like it. Praise God!"*

Now, let's ask ourselves, how would we respond to such a situation? Would we be ready for it? Would we trust God? Would we be willing to risk everything to save our relationship with God? For Daniel he was ready because he prepared ahead of time. Daniel hadn't just started praying to God, it was something he did all the time (vs. 10). He cherished his time with God. Do we? Or do we simply try to fit Him in when and where it's convenient for us? As Brother Lawrence exhorted, *"There's no greater lifestyle and no greater happiness than that of having a continual conversation with God."*

Let us not wait till we're told we can't pray to the Lord for it to mean something to us. Prepare today through prayer for we never know what tomorrow will bring. Whether it be a soldier or an athlete, no one shows up for 'game day' without have practiced and prepared ahead of time. Remember, conviction spurs preparation which breeds unrelenting faith. Martin Luther put it so well when he said, *"Faith is the 'yes' of the heart, a conviction on which one stakes one's life."* Prepare today and anticipate how God will change those roaring lions into cuddly kittens.

Food for Thought

What types of 'punishment' am I willing to endure to continue my relationship with God?

_____

_____

_____

_____

_____

When I am gone, what will others say about my relationship with God?

_____

_____

_____

_____

_____

Today the world is looking for someone to stand for Christ. How am I taking this stand daily in my sphere of influence? Be specific.

_____

_____

_____

_____

_____

Is my daily faith walk preparing me for the challenges that lie ahead? If not, how can I strengthen it?

_____

_____

_____

_____

_____

It's easy to speak for Christ around other believers. It's even relatively easy to speak for Christ in a free land. However, do my words match my actions? And, would I be willing to continue to speak for Christ under persecution? How can I be sure?

_____

_____

_____

_____

_____

✝

Week 51
RAGS TO RICHES

Now you are no longer a slave but God's own child.
And since you are his child, God has made you his heir.
- Galatians 4:7

As per an article in the Los Angeles Times years ago, Bill Cruxton was an old man enjoying his twilight years. He frequented the same restaurant near his hometown in Chagrin Falls in Ohio on a weekly basis. Each visit he made sure to sit at the table in the same section. The waitress, Cara Wood, a friendly and outgoing teenager, manned that section. She always took time to serve Mr. Cruxton and to run errands for the old man. On occasion she would even willingly go to his place to help with household chores. For Cruxton, Cara was not only his favorite waitress, she was also his best friend. When he passed away at the age of 82 in 1992, Cara was named the sole beneficiary of Cruxton's entire estate.

The story depicted in the previous paragraph paints so well the picture of the Christian life and the eternal inheritance promised. The waitress and the customer did not have simply a professional relationship; it was a friendship. They enjoyed each other's company so that they would go out of their way to help each other and to have time to fellowship. Even more, they had become 'family'; not through blood but through conscience choice. This relationship had become so entrenched and solidified that upon Cruxton's death, he was willing and wanting to leave all of his possessions to Wood. This illustration demonstrates how God through Jesus has bestowed upon us His eternal riches. In fact, when one places his faith and trust in Christ as his personal Savior, he not only becomes forgiven and promised a home in Heaven, saved from eternal damnation in Hell, but he becomes a co-heir with Christ.

We read in Romans 8:17, *"And since we are his children, we are his heirs. In fact, together with Christ we are heirs of God's glory."* Think about what this verse means. As breathtaking and overwhelming as it must have been for Cara Wood when she was notified of the unimaginable wealth she had inherited, this wealth was at the same time temporal. It would eventually be gone and she would not be able to take it with her. Contrary, God's riches to us ward are expansive, unending and eternal. When you consider how this young woman's life changed on a dime; how she most certainly went from a life of living week to week to now having been able to pay off her debts and still have more than she had ever known, and then you translate that to how a man's life changes when he accepts Christ, there really is no comparison. It would absolutely be enough if all that we received upon accepting Christ was to be spared an eternity in the flames of hell but we are promised and given so much more.

We are promised to have Christ walk this life with us while many times He carries us. Our ledger has been cleared of all debts and now reflects indescribable wealth. We are no longer dead in sin but alive in Christ. We are no longer at enmity with God but are now His children. We are no longer considered servants but friends. We are promised a home in Heaven where we will be afforded with a personal mansion. We will be rewarded for having the privilege of serving our King. We will have the pleasure of praising Christ for all of eternity knowing we will never sorrow or shed another tear. We are given, not just life, but abundant life!

During the 1980's, there was a television show called Rags to Riches. The show's concept centered around a street-wise, New Jersey born self-made millionaire who adopts five orphan girls. In order to improve his own image and benefit his position economically, the millionaire perpetuates the embellished lie by preying upon the emotions of five girls he reads about in the local newspaper who refuse to become separated. His plan is to move them to his mansion in Bel Air long enough for him to close a business deal. However, after getting to know the girls the story ends with a happy resolution as he adopts the girls and they trade their lives at the orphanage for the lap of luxury.

Aren't you glad that God doesn't, nor has He ever, had an ulterior motive for loving us and showering His blessings upon us? God's love is pure and unconditional. He loves us and simply desires a relationship with us. It is not something we have to earn or even could; it is simply the generous, loving persona of the Almighty God. Romans 5:8 tells us, *"But God showed his great love for us by sending Christ to die for us while we were still sinners."* We don't deserve it but praise God He loves us despite our condition. Like all orphans and outcasts, what a blessing to know we no longer live in poverty but to the contrary are children of the King and co-heirs with Jesus Himself!

Food for Thought

Am I positively affecting others' lives for the better or the worse? When I'm gone, what will I be remembered for?

_____

_____

_____

_____

_____

Name 3 ways that Christ's saving grace has changed my life. Be specific.

_____

_____

_____

_____

_____

As a child of the Heavenly King, what are the biblical promises I can claim today?

_____

_____

_____

_____

_____

How can I specifically bestow 'eternal riches' on others to demonstrate Christ's love?

_____

_____

_____

_____

As Christ provides unconditional love to everyone, I must consider what type of love I am showing to others. Do I love like Christ or do I love based upon my perspectives? Explain.

_____

_____

_____

_____

_____

✝

Week 52
BATS IN THE ATTIC

Don't let evil conquer you,
but conquer evil by doing good.
- Romans 12:21

Recently our home was diagnosed with home intruders, an uninvited irritation living in our attic – bats. After researching how and what was necessary to rid ourselves of this problem and learning how costly and difficult the process would be, it was evident this was an attack by the wicked one. Let us back up for just a moment and better understand the reason I make this accusation.

Over the previous two years I had begun writing. God was giving me the thoughts to pen and the material to flesh out these messages. In addition, He continued to groom my skills so as to be coherent, relative and impactful in presenting God's word to a world hurting and in turmoil. During this process He had begun to instill in my heart the need to present and publish so as to impact others on a grander scale. During this time, He had also provided brothers and sisters to encourage and act as His reinforcing factor that this was the direction I was to follow. So over the last 6 months I had been praying for guidance and wisdom in searching for the right connection that would allow this desire to come to fruition. Approximately a month previous to the 'bat channel' God answered this prayer and united our hearts together with one who will help us carry God's word to many in dire need.

Christians today are often unprepared and ill-equipped when the enemy begins his assault because we have rarely done anything to give the enemy cause to notice us.

As a family we decided to step out by faith and pursue the publishing option. And that is when Satan mounted his attack. It is no coincidence that we would begin to be hampered in our pursuit to follow God's leading. The devil is never concerned with one until he decides to get involved, become active and follow God's calling. At that time, one should expect to have the full fury of hell unleashed against him. The attacks will come hard, fast and furious; and they will be cloaked in a mass of different methods, from financial to emotional to physical to spiritual. Be sure that when you decide to engage in the battle we are all called to, you will face opposition, adversity and an onslaught like you never imagined. This my friends, is the time to honker down, entrench oneself in the Word and prayer, and take the battle to enemy.

Christians today are often unprepared and ill-equipped when the enemy begins his assault because we have rarely done anything to give the enemy cause to notice us. American Christians, in particular, live a life of relative ease and comfort, both physically and spiritually. While society attempts to rid the culture and social arena of all Godly influences, for the individual believer, we are still unimpeded in our faith and practices. We attend church whenever we desire. We attend whatever church we desire. We have the ability to pray whenever and wherever we choose. We are able to verbally share our faith with others – although there is a push to restrict when, where and how we can do this. We are able to vote based upon biblical convictions and for those who most closely represent those principles. In a nation that has so much religious freedom, one must consider whether he is taking advantage of the opportunities at his feet or has he become fat and lazy, lethargic and complacent, apathetic and indifferent?

Throughout the Church age it is no secret that Christianity has surged under persecution; however, the ability to stand under persecution requires a level of spiritual stamina often experienced by a relative few. In the book of Acts, where the early Church originated, Christians experienced persecution under the Roman Empire by the thousands, being fed to lions, stoned, burned alive (primarily as torches for Nero's garden) and many other gruesome measures. One particular stalwart of the early Church was Stephen. Also believed to be one of the first deacons in the Church. Stephen would lose his life at the hands of a stoning for refusing to back down from sharing the truth of the Gospel in the midst of a raucous and deviant political system. Then there is John the Baptist who would literally lose his head over a woman. Because John continued to preach the Gospel and shine light on illicit adulterous relationships, his head was requested as a gift from the king. In addition to these two men, there was Polycarp who is believed to have been instrumental in the compilation of the New Testament. After refusing to burn incense to the Roman Emperor, he was sentenced to burn at the stake; however, as this did not kill him, he was therefore stabbed to death.

Then there is John Wycliffe who lived during the fourteenth century. Possibly Wycliffe's most impactful contribution to the Gospel was translation of the scriptures into common English. As the Catholic Church thought it not enough to simply murder him, his body was exhumed and burned along with many of his writings. Along these lines, William Tyndale stood against many false doctrines of the Catholic Church and against the sexual indiscretions of King Henry VIII costing him his life through strangulation and then the burning of his dead body. As exemplified and recorded as historical facts, believers who have been willing to stand against the immorality and sin of this world and to cry out for the gospel and godly righteousness have often met their demise at the hands of ungodly men. When one decides to stand for Christ, the devil will no longer sit back unaffected; he will come at you with barrels loaded, holding nothing back.

This by no means indicates that a believer should be unnerved or intimidated; but what it does mean is that we ought to be aware of the consequences of standing for Christ. For when one is conscientious of his decisions, it prepares him for the known and unknown, allowing him to be battle tested and equipped for the contest. Additionally, a believer need only to remember that the battle is not ours, it's Christ's and He's already won it. We find our strength, our perseverance, our determination and ultimately, our victory in Him. While it is true that at times it may cost our lives, all the time it will cost us something. For he who is not ready to be engaged in war maybe the solution is to not get into the fight; however, for him who chooses to slink away and avoid the hellish aggression, just remember Christ's words found in Matthew 10:33, *"But everyone who denies me here on earth, I will also deny before my Father in heaven."* Instead soldier of the cross, press on. As it's also written in Matthew 16:25, *"If you try to hang on to your life, you will lose it. But if you give up your life for my sake, you will save it."* As D.L. Moody once noted, *"Let God have your life; He can do more with it than you can."*

Today be reminded that when you choose to do something mighty for God, you will place a bullseye on your back. The devil will bring everything he's got to prevent and destroy you. But also remember that *"...the Spirit who lives in you is greater than the spirit who lives in the world."* Beth Moore was once quoted as saying, *"Every inch of ground we refuse to take with God, we surrender to the enemy."* - I John 4:4. The battle is already won – now take possession of the land.

Food for Thought

What 'bats' have recently entered my head and attacked my plans for Christ?

_____

_____

_____

_____

_____

Do I believe that Christ will provide so as to step out by faith or am I remaining stifled in my faith? Be specific.

_____

_____

_____

_____

_____

If the 'bats' were to be removed, what would I do for Christ today? Be specific.

_____

_____

_____

_____

_____

Statistically goals have a much higher percentage of achievement when written down. List 3 goals for my faith walk over the next 6 months.

_____

_____

_____

_____

_____

Cite how my world will be closer to Christ because of my willingness to contend for the faith.

_____

_____

_____

_____

_____

About Dave

Dave is a husband, father, author, but most of all, disciple of Christ. He was raised in a Christian home and accepted Christ as my personal Savior at the young age of 6 years old. Over the course of his life, he has experienced highs and lows just as any other believer. However, through it all, God has never given up on him.

In 1989 he went to college at Liberty University where he started as a ministry major. Due to experiences, both internal and external, he left college after two years. After returning home and beginning a career in retail management, he met his better half and soon married her. Almost three years after marrying Lindsey, God blessed them with their first, of ultimately four, sons. Dave began moving through and advancing within his field – however never feeling completely fulfilled.

After having been away from school for nearly 15 years God opened an opportunity for him to go back to school. He graduated Liberty University with a Bachelor's of Science in Business Management. Standing on the field at graduation he recall telling his family how he felt God calling him to serve Him there, so they started praying, pursuing, and continuing his Graduate education. After almost 4 years in this pursuit and wondering if it was ever going to happen, Dave received a call from Liberty University; after a few interviews, he was offered a position.

Now his family would once again step out by faith, moving over 400 miles from our families and friends, and starting over. It was quite a challenge and struggle, both emotionally, physical, spiritually, and financially. But God continued to provide. Dave graduated from Liberty with a Master's in Business Administration with a specialization in Leadership. Roughly two years into his tenure at Liberty University he began writing. The dream of writing had been placed on his heart years earlier but he never knew how that would occur or what it would look like. To be honest, he was always discouraged by the negativity on Facebook so he felt led to provide positive, God-driven content – which led him to begin writing devotionals. Over the last few years God has taught him much, in his own spiritual walk and in how to be an author. Dave has several books currently in production and is speaking on how to be strong in Faith. If you would like to talk with Dave or plan a workshop for his teachings please follow his Battlestrong Ministries group on Facebook, reach out to him at 609-709-4967 or visit his website at www.BattlestrongMinistries.com.

Made in the USA
Middletown, DE
15 December 2016